The Simple Way to Study the Book of

Revelation

AUGUSTE GARY

WESTBOW
P R E S S®
A DIVISION OF THOMAS NELSON
& ZONDERVAN

WestBow Press books may be ordered through booksellers or by contacting:

WestBow Press
A Division of Thomas Nelson & Zondervan
1663 Liberty Drive
Bloomington, IN 47403
www.westbowpress.com
1 (866) 928-1240

ISBN: 978-1-5127-1882-9 (sc)
ISBN: 978-1-5127-1883-6 (e)

Library of Congress Control Number: 2015918409

Print information available on the last page.

WestBow Press rev. date: 11/10/2015

Table of contents

Chapter 5

Chapter 6

Introduction

The material presented in this book is a thorough study that is based entirely on the wisdom and the self-sufficiency of the word of God. The subjects such as the **Deity of the Lord Jesus**, the **wisdom of the seven letters to the seven Churches**, the **mystery** of the **Rapture of the Church**, the **redemption plan of God**, and the **judgment of the great tribulation** are all explained in the simplest possible manner.

Each one of those topics that are covered in this study provides a piece of information that reveals the separation between the **Church age** and the period of the **great tribulation**. The literal parts of the book of Revelation are not included in this study. But everything that has to do with the *symbols*, the *structure*, and the *spiritual language* of the book of Revelation is meticulously explained in conformity with the wisdom of the scriptures. This study has absolutely nothing to do with intellectual knowledge, but it has all to do with the **spiritual blessings** of the Church.

We strongly encourage you to verify everything that is said in this study in light of the word of God, and we also encourage you to pay close attention to the details that are provided in this study regarding the difference between the **Church age** and the **seven-year tribulation**.

Chapter 1

To begin with our study of the book of Revelation, the first two **basic aspects** we are going to take into consideration are the followings:

1. The **way** the messages are **organized**
2. The **way** the messages are **communicated**

How are the messages of the book of Revelation organized?

The messages of the book of Revelation are **divided** into two separate parts:

1

A message about the Lord Jesus and his **Church**; **(Revelation 1-3)**

2

A message about the Lord Jesus and his **judgment**; **(Revelation 4-22)**

How are the messages of the book of Revelation communicated?

The messages of the book of Revelation are communicated both in a **literal** (*80%*) and a **symbolic** (*20%*) way. Some of the **symbols** of the book of Revelation are already interpreted in the book itself, but most of them are not. All of those symbols that are not explained in the messages of the book of Revelation can easily be interpreted through the other prophetic books, such as, but not limited to, *Isaiah, Ezekiel, Daniel, and Zechariah*.

To understand the book of Revelation in its entirety, all you need is a **clear** and an **accurate** interpretation of the **symbols** that are incorporated into the **literal messages**. Once you understand the correct way to interpret the messages that are conveyed through the **structure**, the **symbols,** and the **spiritual expressions** of the book of Revelation, you will no longer have any difficulty understanding the messages of the book of Revelation in a complete manner. The Lord did not send those messages to his people in order to confuse them, but rather, to open their eyes on the hidden things of God. The book of Revelation is a blessing to God's people. The more you understand its messages, the more it'll open your eyes on the reality of the **Rapture of the Church**.

Please remember, the book of Revelation is a *very simple* and a *very well-organized* book. The most effective way to study the messages of that book is to stay in the simplicity of the word of the Lord. Everything that is said in that book was placed there for a purpose.

The introduction of the Apostle John
(Revelation, chapter 1, verse: 1-9)

Revelation 1:1-2: "The Revelation of Jesus Christ, which God gave unto him, to shew unto his servants things which **must shortly come to pass**; and he sent and signified it by his angel unto his servant John: 2 Who bare record of the word of God, and of the testimony of Jesus Christ, and of all things that he saw. (*See Rev 4:1, 5:1-10*)

Here is where you need to start paying attention to the truthfulness of the **Rapture of the Church** when you begin studying the book of Revelation.

The purpose for which the *judgment of the great tribulation* was revealed to the Church is clearly explained in the above passage. As you can see, the judgment of the great tribulation was not revealed to God's people as an announcement of what they will have to suffer in the future. This is not what the Revelation of the Lord was about at all. If the Church of Jesus-Christ really had anything to do with the judgment of *the great tribulation*, the Lord Jesus would have overtly revealed it to the Church just like he did in the letter to the Church of Smyrna, because the tribulation of the Church has never been kept secret from the Church.

Rev 2:10: "*Fear none of those things which thou shalt **suffer**: behold, the devil shall cast some of you into prison, that ye may be tried; and ye shall have **tribulation** ten days: be thou faithful unto death, and I will give thee a crown of life*".

The words of blessing of the Apostle John:

Revelation 1:3: "Blessed is he who reads and those who hear the words of this prophecy, and keep those things which are written in it; <u>**for the time is near**</u>".

> Here, John was quoting the words of the Lord Jesus.

Revelation 22:7: "7 Behold, I come quickly: blessed is he that keepeth the sayings of the prophecy of this book". (*The Lord Jesus*)

If the Church of God will have to suffer the judgment of the great tribulation, then why has the Lord Jesus promised a blessing to those who **read** the words of the prophecy? How can the judgment of the disobedient be a **blessing** to God's people? Will God judge his Church with the world?

Absolutely not! The Church of God **bears** and **shares** the suffering that the Lord Jesus went through in this world for his Church, but the judgment of the great tribulation is the punishment that God will repay to the world for **rejecting** the forgiveness of his Son. The Church will not suffer with the world, because she is already in the midst of the suffering of Christ.

2 Thessalonians 1:6: "seeing it is a righteous thing with God to **recompense** tribulation to them that trouble you; 7 and to you who are troubled rest with us, when the Lord Jesus shall be revealed from heaven with his mighty angels, 8 in flaming fire **taking vengeance** on them that know not God, and that obey not the gospel of our Lord Jesus Christ".

(See Revelation 19:11-21)

The **vengeance** that Paul is talking about here will begin with the **seven-year tribulation** and will end with the **judgment of the nations**. (Matt 25:31)

4

The seven spirits which are before the throne of God

Revelation 1:4-5: "4 John to the seven churches which are in Asia: **Grace** be unto you, and **peace**, from him **which is**, and **which was**, and **which is to come**; and from **the seven Spirits** which are before his throne;

5 And from Jesus Christ, who is the faithful witness, and the first begotten of the dead, and the prince of the kings of the earth. Unto him that loved us, and washed us from our sins in his own blood" (*See also 2 John 1:1-3*)

Who are those seven spirits? Are they angels?

Those *seven spirits* which are mentioned in the above verses are not angels. The Apostle John would have never committed the sin of putting **the angels** of God in a position of equality with God. It is only God, in the persons of the **Father**, the **Son**, and the **Holy Spirit**, who has the power to grant to his Church the blessings of his **Grace** and **peace**.

To understand the reason why the expression "**the seven spirits**" was used by the Apostle John in reference to the person of the **Holy Spirit**, you need to remember that the writing of **John's introduction** was based entirely on the things that are mentioned in the Revelation of the Lord Jesus. Those **seven spirits** that the Apostle John is talking about in his **introduction** were revealed to him in the vision of **Revelation, chapter 4.**

Revelation 4:5: "and out of the throne proceeded lightnings and thunderings and voices: and there were **seven lamps of fire** burning before the throne, *which are the* **seven Spirits of God**".

5

Also, in **Revelation 5:6,** we read the following: "And I beheld, and, lo, in the midst of the throne and of the four beasts, and in the midst of the elders, stood a **Lamb** as it had been slain, having **seven horns** and **seven eyes**, which are **the seven Spirits of God**, *sent forth into all the earth*".

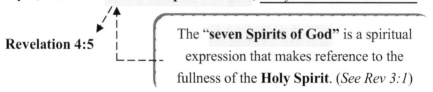

Revelation 4:5

The "**seven Spirits of God**" is a spiritual expression that makes reference to the fullness of the **Holy Spirit**. (*See Rev 3:1*)

"Sent forth into all the earth" ---- When the Apostle John was taken up to the throne room of Heaven, he did not actually see a physical manifestation of the **seven spirits** of the Lord Jesus. The **seven lamps of fire**, as well as the **seven horns** and the **seven eyes** of the Lamb were only revealed to John as a symbol of the Spirit who was sent on the earth on the *day of Pentecost.*

The expression the "seven Spirits of God" was first mentioned by the Lord Jesus in *Revelation 3:1*, and that same expression was then repeated by the Apostle John in Revelation *4:5 and 5:6.* Without the interpretation of the Apostle John, it would have been totally impossible for us to understand what the **seven lamps of fire**, the **seven eyes** and the **seven horns** of the Lamb really mean in the context of the book of Revelation.

Remember: the **seven spirits** of the **Lamb** (Jesus-Christ) do not represent *seven angels of Revelation 8*. Whether you say the **seven spirits of God** or the **seven spirits of the Lamb**, they all mean the same thing, because the Lamb of God is equal to God. The Lord Jesus is the one who possesses the **fullness** of the **Holy Spirit** who is also called the **seven spirits of God** (*See Revelation 3:1, John 1:14-16*). *The message is as simple as that.*

The three persons of the Godhead

In the *salutation* of the Apostle John, *the three persons* of the Godhead are mentioned at the same time, but the only person who is identified by a proper name is the **second person** of the Godhead. The name of **Jesus-Christ** is the very name of God, in which is revealed both the **humanity** and the **Divinity** of God. Throughout the book of Revelation, the **Divinity** and the **Lordship** of **Jesus-Christ** are revealed through the **position of authority**, the **attributes**, and the **titles** that he shares with **God the Father**.

For example, in the salutation of *Revelation 1:4-6*, the Apostle John refers to **God the Father** as the one *who is, who was, and who is to come*. Then in the **8**[th] *verse* of the same introduction, he uses the same expression in reference to the person of the Lord Jesus.

Verse 8: "**Behold, he cometh** with clouds; and every eye shall see him, and they also **which pierced him**: and all kindreds of the earth shall wail because of him. Even so, Amen". [8] **I am Alpha** and **Omega**, the **beginning** and the **ending**, <u>**saith the Lord**</u>, *which is*, and *which was*, and *which is to come*, **the Almighty**.

The Apostle John did not hear those words from God the Father, but rather, he simply repeated what he heard from the *Lord Jesus*: "**12** and, behold, **I come quickly**; and my reward is with me, to give every man according as his work shall be. **13 I am Alpha** and **Omega**, the **beginning** and the **end**, the first and the last". *(Revelation 22:12-13)*

The Divinity of Jesus is the key message of the Revelation of God.

Chapter 2

The Lord Jesus in the midst of the Seven golden candlesticks

Revelation 1:9-20

Revelation 1:9-10: "[9] I John, who also am your brother, and companion in tribulation, and in the kingdom and patience of Jesus Christ, was in the isle that is called Patmos, for the word of God, and for the testimony of Jesus Christ. [10] *I was in the Spirit* **on the Lord's Day**, and heard behind me a great voice, as of a trumpet".

What did the Apostle John mean exactly by the expression "**on the Lord's Day**"? Was he referring to the **first day of the week** or was he referring to the **Judgment Day**? - To find out which one of those two interpretations is correct, first of all, let's take a look at the following **comparison**:

① Here is what is said in the passage of Revelation 1:10: "*I was in the Spirit* **on the Lord's Day**, and heard behind me a great voice, as of a **trumpet**" 11 saying, I am Alpha and Omega, the first and the last: and, What thou seest, write in a book, and send it unto the seven churches which are in Asia; unto **Ephesus**, and unto **Smyrna**, (........)

As you can see from this comparison, the **vision** that was given to John in Rev 1:10 had nothing to do with the **Judgment of the great tribulation.**

② Now here is said in the passage of Revelation 4:1-2: "1 **After** this I looked, and, behold, a door was opened in heaven: and the first voice which I heard was as it were of a **trumpet** talking with me; which said, Come up hither, and I will shew thee things which must be hereafter. 2 **And immediately** *I was in the spirit*: and, behold, a throne was set in heaven, and one sat on the throne.

If the Apostle John was really talking about the **Judgment Day** when he used the expression "**on the Lord's Day**", he would have certainly put it in the same way he had expressed it in the passage of **1 John 4:17-18**:

Verses 17-18: "17 Herein is our love made perfect, that we may have boldness in the **Day of Judgment**: because as he is, so are we in this world. 18 There is no fear in love; but perfect love casteth out fear: because fear hath torment. He that feareth is not made perfect in love".

There is absolutely no doubt it; the expression "**on the Lord's Day**" is indeed a reference to the *first day of week*. Because, as you have just seen in the preceding comparison, the judgment of the **great tribulation** was revealed to John <u>after</u> he was finished recording the **vision of chapter 1:10-20** and the **seven messages** to the seven Churches. The Apostle John did not receive all the messages of the book of Revelation in just one **single vision.**

The message of the 7 golden candlesticks
(Revelation 1:12-20)

Revelation 1:12-20: "[12] And I turned to see the voice that spake with me. And being turned, I saw **seven golden candlesticks**; [13] and in the midst of the seven candlesticks one like unto the Son of man, clothed with":

1. A garment down to the foot, and girt about the paps with a **golden girdle.**
2. His **head** and his **hairs** were white like wool, as white as snow
3. and his **eyes** were **as a flame of fire**;
4. and his **feet** like unto fine brass, **as if they burned in a furnace**;
5. And his **voice** as the sound of many waters.
6. And he had in his **right hand** seven stars
7. and out of his **mouth** went **a sharp two-edged sword**
8. And his **countenance** was as the **sun shineth in his strength.**

If there is one thing in the entire book of Revelation that God the Father does not want his people to be mistaken about, it's certainly the **Divine identity** of his Son Jesus-Christ. Every little detail that appears in the passage of *Revelation 1:10-20* carries a piece of information that reveals the **Deity**, the **Lordship** or the **supreme authority** of the Lord Jesus.

- His **garment** and his **golden girdle** depict his majesty
- His **head** and his **white hair** depict him as the **Ancient of days**, like God the Father is described in the vision of *Daniel 7: 9-13-22.*
- Wherever his sets his **feet** is sanctified (*See Exodus 3:5, Joshua 5:15*)
- His **voice** is the voice of God the Father:

  > **Ezekiel 43:2**: *"And, behold, the glory of the God of Israel came from the way of the east: and his **voice** was like a **noise of many waters**: and the earth shined with his glory".*

- With **his right hand** *he protects*, *he leads*, and *he strengthens* his Church through his **shepherds**, by the power of the Holy Spirit.
- The **word of his mouth** is like a *sharp two-edged sword* (a type of the word of judgment of the Lord, or the sword of the Spirit).
- **The glory of his face** depicts the glory of God the Father
- He is the **first** and the **last**, i.e. the Eternal one. (*Isaiah 43:10*)
- **The keys** (*power and authority*) of **hell** and **death** are in his possession. Because of his victory on the cross of Calvary, the powers of Hell and Death no longer have any authority over the redeemed who are delivered from the powers of darkness.

This Jesus who died on the cross of Calvary for the cause of humanity was more than just a man; he was the True Eternal God.

"His **eyes were as a flame of fire**"
"And out of his mouth was a **two-edged sword**"

Just before we get into the details of those two **symbolic images** that are mentioned above, we will invite you to take a look with us at the passage of *Revelation 19:11-15*, so we can better understand the spiritual meaning of the manifestation of the Lord Jesus in the midst of the **seven candlesticks**:

Revelation 19:11-15

"11 And I saw heaven opened, and behold a white horse; and he that sat upon him was called Faithful and True, and in righteousness he doth judge and make war. 12 **His eyes were as a flame of fire**, and on his head were many crowns; and he had a name written, that no man knew, but he himself. 13 And he was clothed with a vesture dipped in blood: and his name is called The Word of God. 14 And the armies which were in heaven followed him upon white horses, clothed in fine linen, white and clean. 15 **And out of his mouth goeth a sharp sword**, that with it he should **smite the nations**: and he shall rule them with a rod of iron: and he treadeth the winepress of the fierceness and wrath of Almighty God".

The eyes of the Lord Jesus are attentive to the **works of his people**, and he's also aware of what is happening among the **heathens**. The way the Lord judges the works of his people is totally different from the way he judges the works of the **heathens**. For example, in the messages to the seven Churches, which we are going to study in the following chapter, the Lord Jesus uses his **sharp two-edged sword** (*his word of judgment*) to judge the *works of his servants*, but he doesn't use his **sword of judgment** against his people.

This is the warning of the Lord Jesus to the Church of Pergamum:

Revelation 2: 15-16: "¹⁵ so hast thou also them that hold the doctrine of the Nicolaitans, which thing I hate. ¹⁶ **Repent**; or else I will come unto thee quickly, and will **fight** against them with the **sword of my mouth**".

The Lord Jesus uses the **sword of his mouth** to *judge* the works of his people, i.e. to separate the **holy** from the **profane** and the **precious** from the **vile**. He **rebukes** and **chastens** his people, but he does not use his **sword of judgment** against his servants. The two-edged sword of the Lord is reserved for his enemies. He will use it to **smite the nations** (*Rev 19:14-15*).

If you can understand the **spiritual message** of the vision of *Revelation 1:10-20* in its spiritual context, it'll also be very easy for you to understand what the **seven messages** to the **seven Churches** of Asia are all about. The message of *Revelation 1:10-20* is communicated in a **visual way** and the message of *Revelation 2-3* is communicated in a **verbal way**, but in terms of their spiritual essence they are all the same.

The Lord Jesus is the **Supreme Judge** who has established by God to judge the world, but when we read **1 Peter 4: 17-18**, it tells us clearly where the judgment of God begins: "17 for the time is come that **judgment** must begin **at the house of God**: and if it first begin at us, what shall the end be of them that **obey not the gospel of God**? 18 And if the righteous scarcely be saved, where shall the **ungodly and the sinner** appear?"

That simple verse all by itself is enough to explain the spiritual meaning of the manifestation of the Lord Jesus in the midst of the **seven candlesticks**.

It is not for no reason that the "**eyes as a flame of fire**" and the "**two-edged sword**" are mentioned both in *Revelation 1:10-20* and *Revelation 19:11-15*. The judgment of the world is yet to come, but the judgment of the Church is happening now because the High Priest of the house of God (*the Church*) is constantly present in the midst of his people.

End of the study of Revelation 1:10-20

Chapter *3*

The seven letters to the seven churches of Asia

I know thy works

The **purpose** and the **wisdom** of the seven letters

This study that we are going to share with you in this third chapter is not intended to explain everything that is said in the seven letters of Revelation. The main objective of this study is to provide you with some useful pieces of information that will serve you well in the reading of the seven letters.

Here are the *three main points* that we are going to address in this chapter:

1. The **literal aspect** of the seven letters
2. The **symbolic** and **prophetic meaning** of the seven Churches
3. And the **general application** of the seven letters

Why should the seven letters of Revelation be taken literally?

Here is the key verse that answers the question:

> **Revelation 1:19:** "Write the things which thou hast seen, and *the things which are*, and *the things which shall be hereafter*;"

As you can see in the above verse, the **seven letters of Revelation** were not split into seven prophetic periods as many people believe it. The "**things**" that were happening in the **seven Churches** were placed in the present, because all of the local Churches are not facing the same challenges at the same time. The idea of saying that the seven letters of Revelation represent *seven prophetic periods in Church history* is completely wrong, because the Lord Jesus never said that. The judgment of the great tribulation is yet to come, but the Church of the Lord (*those who are alive*) is still on the earth.

All of those things that were happening in the seven Churches were written as a prediction of what the spiritual conditions of the Churches would be like throughout the period of the **dispensation of grace**.

The **symbolic** and the **prophetic meaning** of the seven Churches

If you want to understand both the **symbolic** and the **prophetic meaning** of the *seven Churches* of Asia in the general context of the book of Revelation, the very first thing you need to pay attention to is the *frequent repetition* of the number seven, and the second thing you will also need to take into consideration is the *spiritual meaning* of the **number seven**.

Here is how the **number seven** is repeated in the book of Revelation:

The things of the Church	The great tribulation
(Revelation 1-3)	*(Revelation 6-22)*
1. 7 golden candlesticks	1. 7 seals, 7 trumpets, 7 plagues
2. 7 stars	2. 7 thunders, 7 lamps of fire
3. 7 Churches, 7 letters	3. 7 heads of the beast
4. 7 spirits of God	4. 7 angels (2x), etc.

All of those series of sevens that are repeated in the book of Revelation are no different from one another in terms of their *spiritual meanings*. As you already know, the number seven is a number that is usually used in the bible to indicate the **fullness**, the **completion**, or the **perfection** of something that has been or will be accomplished by God. The seven Churches of Asia are no exception to the rule. Those seven Churches were purposely selected as *a* *symbolic picture* of the **fullness** of the **body of Christ** under the dispensation of grace, but in terms of their *prophetic meaning*, they simply serve as an indication that reveals a clear separation between the period of the **dispensation of grace** and the period of the **great tribulation**.

The **Fullness** of the Church	the **Fullness** of the judgment of God
Ephesus	Seven Seals
Smyrna	
Pergamum	
Thyatira	Seven Trumpets
Sardis	
Philadelphia	
Laodicea	Seven Plagues

Prophetically, the **fullness** of the Church of Jesus-Christ is represented both under a **symbolic picture** (*the seven Churches*) and a **spiritual name** (*the bride of the Lamb*). There is absolutely no way we could integrate <u>a small part</u> of the Church into the judgment of the great tribulation, because the Church is nowhere to be found between *chapters 6 and 16*.

The study of the seven messages

This study that we are going to share with you now will be divided into the three following parts: *first of all*, we will begin with the **introductions** of the seven letters at the same time; *secondly*, we will talk about the **purpose** for which those **seven messages** were addressed to the seven Churches; thirdly, we will take a quick look at **seven conclusions** (*the 12 rewards*), and from there, we will address the mystery of the **Rapture of the Church.**

① The seven introductions

As you can see in the list below, nothing has changed so far. The same **message** that we found in the vision of *Revelation 1:10-20* is once again repeated in the **seven introductions** of the seven letters. (*See chapter 2*)

To the Church of Ephesus, the Lord is the one who holds the *seven stars* in his right hand and who walks in the midst of the *seven candlesticks*.

To the Church of Smyrna, he's the *First and the Last*; the one who was *dead* and *came back to life*.

To the Church of Pergamum, he's the one who has *the two-edged sword*.

To the Church of Thyatira, he's the *Son of God* whose *eyes are like a flame of fire* and whose *feet are like fine brass*.

To the Church of Sardis, he's the one who possesses the *seven spirits* of God and the *seven stars*.

To the Church of Philadelphia, the Lord Jesus is the **Holy**, the **True**, the **rightful heir** of the throne of David (*the Key of David*). When he opens, no man can shut, and when shuts, no man can open. *(Isaiah 22:22)*

To the Church of Laodicea: he's the **Amen** (*the one who has the word of approval*). He's the **faithful**, the **true witness** who delivered the message of the kingdom to the satisfaction of God the Father. The beginning of the creation of God, i.e. who existed before anything was created.

The Lord Jesus is the **God**, the **Lord**, and the **Chief Shepherd** of all the Churches. His **titles** and his **Divine attributes** do not vary from one particular Church to another; he is the Lord of the entire body of Christ.

The seven letters of Revelation cannot be separated from one another. Because when the Apostle John was sending those *seven messages* to the seven Churches of Asia, each one of the seven Churches had received all the seven letters at the same time. Each one of the seven Churches was aware of the situations of their sister Churches, because they all had something to learn from and to share with one another. Spiritually speaking, all the seven letters of Revelation represent **one complete** message. It's not for no reason that they are all structured in a similar way.

The similar structure of the seven letters

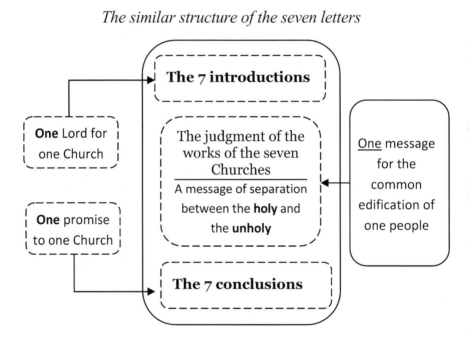

The Chief shepherd of the Church is addressing a message to his people, and he demands that we take heed to the words of his mouth.

---

② The judgment of the works of the seven Churches

It is one thing to read the story of the seven Churches of Asia through the seven letters of Revelation, but it is quite another thing to understand how to read those messages in their *general* and their *spiritual context*. How should we approach the study of the **judgment of the works** of the seven Churches in order to really take advantage of the spiritual lessons that apply to us today? ---- Here is a very simple way we can do that:

To study the **judgment of the works** of the seven Churches, there are three important things we're going to have to take into consideration. **First of all**, we need to pay attention to the shepherds of the seven Churches; **secondly**, we need to look at how the Lord Jesus *deals with* **the situation** of each Church. **And thirdly**, we need to look at how the Lord Jesus **concludes** each one of the seven messages. Those are the *three aspects* that will actually help us understand the **real purpose** of the **seven letters** of Revelation.

The Lord and the seven shepherds

The works of the **shepherds** of the seven Churches were **judged** by the **Chief Shepherd** of the Churches. All the *compliments*, as well as the *blames* were addressed directly and personally to the pastors of the seven Churches, because the solutions to the spiritual problems of a Church begin with the pastor who represents the spiritual authority of his congregation.

"Unto the angel to the Church of Ephesus write: (....), **I know thy works**"

How did the Lord Jesus deal with the situation of each Church?

The message that the Lord Jesus was addressing to the seven Churches of Asia was a message of **warning**; of **encouragement**; of **restoration**; of **repentance**; of **healing**; of **rebuke** and **chastening** for the common good of the believers. That's what the *main purpose* of the seven letters was all about. Although the words of the Lord were very strict, that did not mean he was punishing his servants while they were still in the fight of faith.

As the **High Priest** and the **Chief Shepherd** of the Church, the Lord Jesus did exactly what the word of his Father requires from the shepherds of his flock. He used his **sharp two-edged sword** to separate the **holy** from the **unholy** and the **clean** from the **unclean** (*Ezekiel 22:26*). The Lord Jesus has set an example for us to follow. Not only does he demand that the shepherds be faithful, but he also demands something from the members of his body. The shepherds will not be held accountable for the actions of the flock.

"He that hath an ear, let him hear what the Spirit saith unto the churches"

The Lord Jesus has done pretty much everything necessary to spare his servants from the judgment of the great tribulation. He offers a **blessing** to those who *read*, who *hear*, and who *keep* the things that are written in the word of the prophecy. He reveals the **rewards** that he has in reserve for those who endures until the end. He reveals the atrocities of the judgment of the great tribulation, as well as the judgment of Hell fire, etc. All of those things have been revealed to the Church in advance. Would the Lord Jesus do all that for his servants if he didn't want to spare them? Absolutely not!

When God revealed the judgment of the flood to Noah, he didn't do that because he wanted to judge Noah with the world. Noah was warned by God because he found grace in the eyes of the Lord. (*Genesis 6:8*)

Likewise, the messages of the book of Revelation was also given to the Church as a warning. The Church of Jesus-Christ will not fall under the judgment of the great tribulation with the world. We are now living in a time where people who call themselves Christians are mocking the *promise* of the **Rapture of the Church**. We are living in a time where people who have the word of God in their hands are fighting against the sound doctrine.

What do all of those things mean for the true disciples of Jesus-Christ?

The answer is very simple: the Lord Jesus is at the door. The **great surprise** of *Matthew 24:38-44* is around the corner: " *[44] Therefore be ye also ready: for in such an hour as ye think not the Son of man cometh.*"

The spiritual lessons of the seven letters of Revelation are very clear, very direct, and very simple. What the Lord Jesus demands from us, his people, is that we serve him with a **perfect love** (*Ephesus*); that we remain **faithful** when we are facing *trials* and *tribulations* (*Smyrna*); that we stay away from **spiritual fornication** and **sexual impurity** (*Pergamum*); that we stand against **false doctrine** (*Thyatira*); that we be **vigilant** (*Sardis*) and **zealous** for the spiritual things of the Lord (*Laodicea*). Above all, the Lord demands that we repent of our sins. The **message** that Apostles of the Lord were preaching to the Church of God through the epistles of the New Testament is confirmed through the seven letters of Revelation.

The Church of Laodicea

We don't really think that it would be a good idea at all to conclude this second part of our study without taking a little time to say something about the Church of Laodicea, which, as you already know, is often regarded as an apostate Church that was rejected by the Lord Jesus.

Do you know the vast majority of the members of the body of Christ have such a negative perception about the Church of Laodicea? --- It's simply because they never pay too much attention to the **purpose** for which the *seven letters* were addressed to the seven Churches.

Contrary to the popular belief, the Church of Laodicea was never **rejected** by the Lord Jesus, neither was she presented as an **apostate** Church. The Church of Laodicea was shamefully **rebuked** for her **Lukewarmness** and **chastened** for her **pride**, because she was loved by the Lord Jesus.

> *"As many as I love*, I **rebuke** and **chasten**: be zealous therefore, and repent". (See Hebrews 12:5-8)

The Church of Laodicea was not involved in *sexual perversion*; she was not a *prosperity gospel Church*; she was not an *ecumenical Church*; the pastor of that Church did not fall away from the faith, neither was he involved in false doctrine. The problem of the Church of Laodicea was a problem of *Lukewarmness*, which means that they were not **zealous** for the spiritual things of the Lord, but that did not make them an apostate Church. Are were defending the **Lukewarmness** of the Church of Laodicea? Absolutely not! The Lord Jesus was not pleased with that spiritual condition.

Here is why the Church of Laodicea was **rebuked**:

Revelation 3:15: "I know thy works, that thou art neither cold nor hot: I would thou wert cold or hot. [16] So then **because** thou art lukewarm, and neither cold nor hot, *I will spew thee out of my mouth*".

She was **chastened** for her spiritual pride:

Revelation 3:17: "**Because** thou sayest, *I am rich*, and *increased with goods*, and *have need of nothing*; and knowest not that thou art **wretched**, and **miserable**, and **poor**, and **blind**, and **naked**: [18] I counsel thee to buy of me **gold** tried in the fire, that thou mayest be rich; and **white raiment**, that thou mayest be clothed, and that the **shame of thy nakedness** do not appear; and **anoint thine eyes** with eyesalve, that thou mayest see".

The Church of Laodicea had become lukewarm because somewhere along the line, they had stopped seeking the face of the Lord.

The Church of Laodicea had not always been a lukewarm Church

Colossians 4:13-16: "13 For I can testify that he has worked hard for you and for those in **Laodicea** and *Hierapolis*. 14 Our dear friend Luke the physician and Demas greet you. 15 Give my greetings to the brothers and sisters who are in **Laodicea** and to Nympha and the church that meets in her house. 16 And after you have read this letter, have it read to **the church of Laodicea**. In turn, read the letter from **Laodicea** as well".

(See also Colossians 2:1)

Was the Apostle Paul talking about a *lukewarm* Laodicea in that passage? *Certainly not*. Did the pastor of the Church of Laodicea spend the rest of his ministry in that spiritual condition, in spite of all of those **warnings** and **promises** that were made to the seven Churches? – *Only God knows*.

The Apostate Churches

As we said earlier, the subject of Apostasy is not discussed at all in the seven letters of Revelation. The Lord Jesus was not talking to any apostate Church, because the Apostate Churches have absolutely nothing to do with the Lord Jesus. If the Church of Laodicea was an apostate Church, she would not have even been mentioned in the book of Revelation. The Lord Jesus did not hold the *symbol* of any apostate pastor in his right hand, and he did not stand in the midst of any apostate Church either.

If you'd like to have a full picture of what the bible says about the subject of apostasy, we would encourage you to read the following passages: *Matthew 24:2-12, 2 Timothy 3:1-5, 2 Timothy 4:3-5*, and *2 Thessalonians 2:3*.

In order for a Church to become apostate, the pastor of that Church has to be separated from the Lord Jesus first. As long as the pastor of a Church is under the control of the Lord Jesus; as long as the **anointing** of the Lord is present in a congregation, that Church will always be recognized as a Church of the Lord. The **Apostate Churches** always **separate themselves** from the Church of God, because they don't belong there.

Please take a look at the following passage:

1 John 2:19: "They went out from us, but they were not of us; for if they had been of us, they would no doubt have continued with us: but they went out, that they might be made manifest that they were not all of us."

Remember the **false Apostles** who stood against the Church of **Ephesus**. The apostate leaders of the apostate Churches are not working for the Lord.

When you are reading the seven letters of Revelation, do not try to focus your attention on the spiritual performance of each Church, but rather, keep your attention focused mainly on the spiritual lessons that are contained in the seven letters. The judgment of the works of the seven Churches was carried out by the Lord Jesus only for the purpose of encouraging the **entire body of Christ** in the fight of faith. Most of the members of the Church of Sardis were **spiritually dead**, and the entire Church of Laodicea was **lukewarm**, but they were all given an opportunity to get right with the Lord.

In spite of all the spiritual challenges that we might be facing in our walk with the Lord, we all have an opportunity to get back on our feet. What the Lord Jesus actually wants for his people is their spiritual healing. That's why he has made himself available to each and every one of us who want to restore our **personal relationship** with him by *prayer* and *supplication*:

*"20 Behold, I **stand at the door**, and knock: if any man hear my voice, and open the door, I will come in to him, and will sup with him, and he with me".*

To him that overcometh, will I....

Remember: the Church of Laodicea had a very serious spiritual problem for which she was **rebuked** and **chastened**, but she was not rejected by the Lord Jesus. Their pastor was in the **right hand** (*under the control*) of the Lord, and their **candlestick** was still in its place. There is a big difference between a *lukewarm Church* and an *apostate Church*. The **Lukewarmness** of the Church of Laodicea is nothing compare to the **abominations** that are taking place in the **apostate Churches** of these last days. The apostate Churches are feasting at the table of the world, but the true Church of the Lord Jesus is suffering in the world because of her faith in the Lord Jesus.

③ The twelve rewards of the Lord Jesus
to him that will come out victorious in the fight of faith

Ephesus: the tree of life

Smyrna: the crown of life

Pergamum: the hidden manna

And a new name on a white stone

> All of those rewards will be granted to **each member** of the body of Christ.

Thyatira: power over the nations; *(during the millennial reign)*

And the morning star

Sardis: a white garment

Philadelphia: a pillar in the temple of God;

The name of God, the name of the New Jerusalem, and the new name of the Lord Jesus will be written on the believer

➤ **Will be preserved from the judgment of the great tribulation**

Laodicea: privilege to sit on the throne of the Lord Jesus.

Revelation 3:10: "Because thou hast kept the word of my patience, I also will keep thee from the **hour of temptation**, which shall come upon **all the world**, to try them that dwell upon the earth".

↑

When the Lord Jesus made that promise to the Church of **Philadelphia**, he knew perfectly well that he was not going to fulfill it in their time, because all of the members of the body of Christ were also included in that promise (*Ephesians 4:4-5*). *Now, here is a very simple question we want to ask you:* when you look at the **twelve rewards** that are listed above, have you noticed anything that is related to the suffering of the great tribulation? No, you won't find any, because the suffering of the great tribulation does not represent the **suffering of Christ** for which the Church will be rewarded.

28

How will the Lord Jesus fulfill the promise of the **rapture**?

1 Thessalonians 4:15-18: "**For** this we say unto you **by the word of** **the Lord**, that **we which are alive** *and* remain unto the coming of the Lord shall not prevent them which are asleep. **16** For the Lord himself shall descend from heaven with a shout, with the voice of the archangel, and with the trump of God: and the **dead in Christ** shall rise first: **17** Then **we which are alive** *and* remain shall be caught up **together** with them in the clouds, to **meet the Lord in the air**: and so shall we ever be with the Lord. **18** Wherefore comfort one another with these words".

The Apostle Paul had received that revelation directly from the Lord Jesus.

When will the Lord Jesus fulfill the promise of the Rapture, and how will he fulfill it?

Matthew 24:36-41: "³⁶ But of that *day* and *hour* knoweth **no man**, no, **not** **the angels** of heaven, but my Father only. **37** But **as the days of Noah** were, so shall also the coming of the Son of man be. **38** For as in the days that were before the flood they were **eating** and **drinking, marrying** and **giving in** **marriage**, until the day that Noah entered into the ark, **39** And knew not until the flood came, and took them all away; so shall also the coming of the Son of man be. **40** Then **shall** *two be in the field*; the **one shall be taken**, and **the other left**. **41** *Two women* shall be grinding at the mill; the **one shall be** **taken**, and **the other left**". (*A picture of the rapture*)

The Lord Jesus prophesied it, but he did not explain it to his disciples.

Will there be a warning before the **Rapture**?

Revelation 3:3: "remember therefore how thou hast received and heard, and hold fast, and repent. If therefore thou shalt not watch, I will come on thee **as a thief**, and *thou shalt not know what hour I will come upon thee*".

↑
└─┤ There will be no warning; the rapture can happen at any moment ┊

What will the **rapture of the Church** mean for the world?

1 Thessalonians 5: 1-3: "1 But of the **times** and the **seasons**, brethren, ye have no need that I write unto you. 2 For yourselves know perfectly that **the day of the Lord** so cometh **as a thief in the night**. 3 For when they shall say, **Peace** and **safety**; then sudden destruction cometh upon them, as travail upon a woman with child; and they shall not escape.

This is a second revelation concerning the mystery of the Rapture

1 Corinthians 15: 50-52: "[50] now this I say, brethren, that flesh and blood cannot inherit the kingdom of God; neither doth corruption inherit incorruption. 51 Behold, I shew you a **mystery**; we shall not all sleep, but we shall all be **changed**, 52 *in a moment, in the twinkling of an eye*, at the last trump: for *the trumpet shall sound*, and the **dead** shall be raised incorruptible, and **we** shall be changed."

①   ↑   ② Those who are **alive** shall be changed

The prophecy of **1 Thessalonians 4:15-18** is repeated a second time.
(*The dead in Christ and those who are alive will leave the earth together*)

Chapter 4

Revelation 4-5

The vision of the throne room of Heaven

A Reminder of the fulfillment of the redemption plan of God

After the Apostle John was finished recording the messages to the seven Churches, he was taken up to Heaven in the spirit. In his description of the vision of the throne room of Heaven, he reported that he saw: *1)* the *throne of God*, *2) a rainbow* around the throne, *3) twenty four elders*, *4) seven lamps of fire, 5) four living creatures, 6)* and a *Lamb* that was slain.

Now, in order to find out what kind of message that God is communicating through those images, the very first thing we will need to take into consideration is the image of the "**Lamb that was slain**". What does the image of the Lamb remind us of? The answer is very simple: the image of the Lamb that was slain reminds us of the **fulfillment** of the **redemption plan** of God through the death of his Son Jesus-Christ.

① What does the image of the rainbow remind us of?

The image of the **rainbow** reminds us of three things:
1. The **judgment of the flood** (*a type of the great tribulation*)
2. **Noah** and **his household** (*8 people: a new beginning*)
3. **Noah's Ark** (*a type of the salvation of God in his Son Jesus-Christ*). (See *Genesis 9:13-16*; *Matthew 24: 36-41*).

Those **8 people** who were saved from the judgment of the flood had become an integral part of the *gradual revelation* of the **redemption plan** of God. The bible tells us, in *Genesis 9*, that after the judgment of the flood, God placed his **bow** (*rainbow*) in the sky as a sign of his **covenant** with Noah and all the creatures of the earth.

② What does the image of the twenty four elders remind us of?

The image of the **24 elders** reminds us of the **Jewish nation** through which the **salvation** of God was offered to the world. The identities of those 24 elders are revealed in the passage of *Revelation 21:10-14:*

*"[10] And he carried me away in the spirit to a great and high mountain, and shewed me that great city, the holy Jerusalem, descending out of heaven from God, [11] having the glory of God: and her light was like unto a stone most precious, even like a jasper stone, clear as crystal; [12] and had a wall great and high, and had **twelve gates**, and at the gates twelve angels, and names written thereon, which are **the names** of **the twelve tribes of the children of Israel**:[13] on the east three gates; on the north three gates; on the south three gates; and on the west three gates. [14] And the wall of the city had **twelve foundations**, and in them the **names** of the **twelve apostles of the Lamb**".*

The **12 tribes of the children of Israel** were placed in the midst of the gentile nations as a light to the nations (*Isaiah 49:6*), and the way they were camped in the wilderness had also revealed the purpose of their presence on the earth. They were positioned at the four corners of the earth just like their names are inscribed on the *12 gates* of the New Jerusalem.

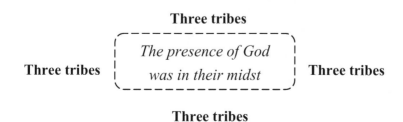

Three tribes

Three tribes   *The presence of God was in their midst*   **Three tribes**

Three tribes

The **12 Apostles of the Lamb** were given the mission to preach the good news of the gospel to the Jews and to all the nations of the earth.

Now, if we take a look at the revelation of the 24 elders from a **prophetic standpoint**, it'll be quite easy to identify the image of the glorified Church, as well as the saints of the Old Testament. The message is as simple as that.

We can't talk about the redemption plan of God without alluding to the nation of Israel, the first born of God among the nations.

"Salvation is from the Jews". (*John 4:22*)

Old Testament	The four gospels	New Testament
The 12 tribes	**Jesus-Christ**	**The 12 Apostles**

③ The seven lamps of fire

Revelation 4:5: "And out of the throne, proceeded lightnings and thunderings and voices: and there were **seven lamps of fire** <u>burning</u> *before the throne,* **which are the seven Spirits of God**". (*See Revelation 1:4-5*)

The image of those **seven lamps of fire** represent a *symbolic picture of* the **Holy Spirit** who ascended upon the Lord Jesus on the day of his water baptism at the Jordan river. When we see the Spirit of the Lord Jesus, we see the life of the **redemption plan of God**.

Revelation 5:6: "6 And I beheld, and, lo, in the midst of the throne and of the four beasts, and in the midst of the elders, stood a **Lamb** as it had been slain, having **seven horns** and **seven eyes, which** **are the seven Spirits of God** sent forth into all the earth."

(See pages 5 and 6)

The faces of the four living creatures

The face of **the lion** presents the Lord Jesus as the **warrior** and the **defender**. The **Lion** of the tribe of Judah who defeated his enemies on the cross of Calvary (*Revelation 5:5, Genesis 49:9-12*).

The face of **the calf** depicts the **submission**, the **patience**, and the **endurance** of Jesus-Christ under the **yoke** of the cross of Calvary as it is written in **Philippians 2:6-8:** *"8 and being found in fashion as a man, he **humbled** himself, and became **obedient** unto death, even the death of the **cross***".

35

The human face reminds us of the **humanity** of Jesus-Christ; the Eternal God who took on flesh for the sake of mankind, according to *1 Timothy 3:16: "¹⁶ And without controversy great is the mystery of godliness: God was manifest in the flesh, justified in the Spirit, seen of angels, preached unto the Gentiles, believed on in the world, received up into glory ".*

The **face of the flying eagle** reminds us of the **exaltation** and the **elevation** of Jesus-Christ after his resurrection from the dead, as it is written in *Philippians 2:5-9: "5 Let this mind be in you, which was also in Christ Jesus: 6 who, being in the form of God, thought it not robbery to be equal with God: 7 but made himself of no reputation, and took upon him the form of a servant, and was made in the likeness of men: 8 and being found in fashion as a man, he humbled himself, and became obedient unto death, even the death of the cross. 9 Wherefore God also hath highly exalted him, and given him a name which is above every name:*

This is one of the characteristics of an eagle:

Obadiah 1:3-4: "3 the pride of thine heart hath deceived thee, (....) 4 Though thou **exalt thyself** as **the eagle**, and though thou **set thy nest** among the stars, thence will I bring thee down, saith the LORD".

Overall, that's what the message of the vision of Revelation 4-5 is all about. The **redemption plan** that was prepared by God since the foundation of the world was gradually revealed throughout the Old Testament period, and then it was fulfilled by the Son of God on the cross of Calvary. The whole burden of mankind was placed upon the shoulders of the Lamb of God.

Chapter 5

The **Anti-Christ** in the prophecies of the **book of Daniel**

An accurate study of the events of the great tribulation is not possible without the prophecies of Daniel.

Daniel 7:1-8, 20-26; 9:20-27; 12:11-12

If it is **possible** to *read* the judgment of the seven-year tribulation without the book of Daniel, it is totally **impossible** to accurately *understand* the fulfillment of that judgment without the **prophecies** which were given in the book of Daniel, in the following order:

- The dream of **king Nebuchadnezzar** (*Daniel 2:29-35*)
- The vision of the **four world Kingdoms** (*Daniel 7:1-8*)
- And the vision of **70 weeks of Daniel** (*Daniel 9:20-27*)

The **interpretation** of king Nebuchadnezzar's dream was revealed to him by Daniel in the following terms:

Daniel 2:29: "As for thee, O king, *thy thoughts came into thy mind* upon thy bed, **what should come to pass hereafter**: and he (*God*) that revealeth secrets maketh known to thee *what shall come to pass*".

Verse 31: "Thou, O king, sawest, and behold a great image. This great image, whose brightness was excellent, stood before thee; and the form thereof was terrible".

1. This image's *head* was of **fine gold (Babylonian empire)**
2. His *breast* and his *arms* of **silver (Medo-Persian empire)**
3. His *belly* and his *thighs* of **brass (Greek empire)**
4. His *legs* of **iron (Roman empire**; *East and West*)

---

5. His *feet* part of **iron** and part of **clay**. (**two feet** and **10 toes**)

↑

This is the last world kingdom.

The **10 toes** represent the **10 kings** who will *reign with* the Anti-Christ.

(*The interpretation of the dream is found in* **verses 36-45**)

38

② The vision of the four world Kingdoms

Daniel 7:1-8: "1 in the first year of Belshazzar king of Babylon Daniel had a dream and visions of his head upon his bed: then he wrote the dream, and told the sum of the matters. 2 Daniel spake and said, I saw in my vision by night, and, behold, the four winds of the heaven strove upon the great sea. 3 And **four great beasts** came up from the sea, diverse one from another".

See Revelation 13:1-18

1. The *first* was **like a lion**, and had eagle's wings:
2. And behold another beast, a *second*, **like to a bear**
3. After this I beheld, and lo another, **like a leopard**, which had **four wings** of a fowl and **four heads**.

Here is the fourth Kingdom**:**

"After this I saw in the night visions, and behold a fourth beast, **dreadful** and **terrible**, and **strong exceedingly**; and it had great iron teeth: it devoured and brake in pieces, and stamped the residue with the feet of it: and it was **diverse** from all the beasts that were before it; and it had **ten horns**. (**10 kings**)

I considered **the horns**, and, behold, there came up among them another **little horn** (*the Anti-Christ*), before whom there were three of the first horns plucked up by the roots: and, behold, in **this horn** were eyes like the eyes of man, and a *mouth speaking great things*". (*See Rev 13*)

Note: In the interpretation of king Nebuchadnezzar's dream, the emphasis was placed on the **10 kings**, but now in the vision of Daniel, the emphasis is placed both on the **Anti-Christ** and the **10 kings**.

The interpretation of the fourth beast

Daniel 7:23-26: "23 Thus he said, The **fourth beast** shall be the fourth kingdom upon earth, which shall be diverse from all kingdoms, and shall devour the whole earth, and shall tread it down, and break it in pieces. 24 And the **ten horns** out of this kingdom are **ten kings** that shall arise: and **another** shall rise after them; and he shall be diverse from the first, and he shall subdue three kings." (*Please remember to read the whole chapter*)

"25 and **he** (*the little horn*) shall speak great words against the most High, and shall wear out the **saints** of the most High, and think to change **times and laws**: and they shall be given into his hand until **a time** and **times** and the **dividing of time**. [26] But the judgment shall sit, and they shall take away his dominion, to consume and to destroy it unto the end".

Now, here are the most important pieces of information you will need to remember from Nebuchadnezzar's dream and Daniel's vision:

- The last world kingdom will begin with **10 kings**
- The **Anti-Christ** will appear under the reign of those *10 kings*
- The Anti-Christ will **subdue three** of those *10 kings* (**Rev 17:12**)
- And he will persecute the Jews for a period of *"A **time**, **times**,* and the *dividing of time* (*See Revelation 12:13-14*)

Note: the period of "*A **time**, **times**, and a **dividing of time**"* is equal to a total of $3^{1/2}$ years. This length of time, which concerns the children of Israel, will be fulfilled exactly during the **second half** of the *seven-year tribulation*. Let us now move on to the prophecy of the 70 weeks of Daniel.

The vision of the 70 weeks of Daniel
(Daniel 9: 24-27)

If you would like to know why the events of the great tribulation will be fulfilled over a period of **7 years**, this prophecy will give you the answer.

The prophetic message of the angel Gabriel to Daniel:

"[24] **Seventy weeks** are determined upon **thy people** and upon **thy holy city**: To *finish the transgression*, and to *make an end of sins*, and to *make reconciliation for iniquity*, and to *bring in everlasting righteousness*, and to *seal up the vision and prophecy*, and to *anoint the most Holy*".

"25 Know therefore and understand, that *from the going forth of the commandment* **to restore** and **to build** Jerusalem unto the **Messiah** *the Prince* shall be **seven weeks, and threescore** and **two weeks**: the street shall be built again, and the wall, even in troublous times". (**7 + 62**)

"26 And after **threescore and two weeks** (*62 x 7 years*) shall **Messiah be cut off**, but not for himself: and the people of the prince that shall come shall **destroy** the **city** and the **sanctuary**; and the end thereof shall be with a flood, and unto the end of the war desolations are determined. (Matt 24:1-3)

The prophecy was fulfilled in part

1. The order to rebuild the temple was issued by **Cyrus**, king of Persia (*Ezra 1*)
2. The Holy Sonly of God, was anointed of the **Holy Spirit** (*Matt 3:16*)
3. Jesus-Christ was crucified fulfilled after the **69 weeks** (*483 years*)
4. In 70 A.D, the temple of Jerusalem was destroyed by the **Roman Empire** (*the fourth kingdom*) as it was prophesied in *Daniel 9:27* and *Matthew 24: 1-3*. The **70th week** *(last 7 years) is yet to be fulfilled?*

What will happen during the **70th** week (*the last 7 years*)?

"²⁷ And **he** shall **confirm the covenant** with many for **one week**: and **in the midst of the week** he shall cause the **sacrifice** and the **oblation** to **cease**, and for the overspreading of abominations he shall make it desolate, even until the consummation, and that determined shall be poured upon the desolate".

According to the above verse, the **Anti-Christ** will sign a **seven-year covenant** with the **Jewish leaders**:

During the first **3 ½ years** The Jews will **at peace** with the Anti-Christ.	During the second **3 ½ years** The Jews will be persecuted by the Anti-Christ. (**Dan 7:25**)

Now, here is a very simple summary on the **three prophecies** that are found in the book of Daniel:

- The final world kingdom will begin with **10 kings**
- The **Anti-Christ** will appear during the reign of those *10 kings*
- The Anti-Christ will **subdue three** of those *10 kings* (**Rev 17:12**)
- At the beginning of his reign, the man of sin will sign a **seven-year covenant** with the Leaders of the nation of Israel.
- In the midst of the seven-years, he will break the covenant, and during the whole **second 3 ^{1/2} years**, he will persecute the Jews.

Overall, those are the key details that we need to take into account before we get into the study of the events of the great tribulation.

This is yet another prophecy that was given by the Apostle Paul concerning the desecration of the temple of God during the seven-year tribulation:

2 Thessalonians 2:3-4: " [3] Let no man deceive you by any means: for *that day shall not come,* except there come a falling away first, and that **man of sin** be revealed, the **son of perdition**; [4] who opposeth and **exalteth himself** above all that is called God, or that is worshipped; so that he as God sitteth **in the temple of God**, shewing himself that he is God".

The temple that the Apostle Paul is talking about here refers to the one that is mentioned in *Revelation 11:1-2.*

What will happen after the desecration of the third temple?

Daniel 12:11-12: "And **from the time** that **the daily sacrifice** shall be taken away, and the **abomination** that maketh desolate **set up**, there shall be *a thousand two hundred and ninety days*. 12 Blessed is he that waiteth, and cometh to the *thousand three hundred and five and thirty days.*

1290 days are equivalent to **44 months** (*3 $^{1/2}$ years + 2 months*) according to the Lunar calendar. **1335 days** are equivalent to **45 $^{1/2}$ months** (*3 $^{1/2}$ years + 3 $^{1/2}$ months*) according to the Jewish calendar.

Please, do not be confused by those two separate numbers; they are all the same. All you need to take into account is the mention of the **1335 days**. If someone told you that he will give you $10, then all of a sudden he tells you that he will give you $12, he simply means that you will receive $2 more.

The seven-year tribulation will be divided into two equal parts of *42 months* (3 $^{1/2}$ years), but there will also be an additional *3 $^{1/2}$ months.*

43

Chapter 6

The opening of the seven seals

Revelation 6-18

The Lord Jesus and his judgment

The judgment of the great tribulation

To begin with the study of the judgment of the seven-year tribulation, the very first thing we are going to have to take into account is the **last prophetic week** (*last 7 years*) of Daniel, *chapter 9:27*:

Daniel 9:27: "And he shall confirm the covenant with many for **one week**"

```
┌─────────────────────────┐  ┌─────────────────────────┐
│ During the first 3 ½ years │  │ During the second 3 ½ years │
│ The Jews will be at peace with │  │ The Jews will be persecuted │
│ the Anti-Christ. │  │ by the Anti-Christ. │
└─────────────────────────┘  └─────────────────────────┘
```

And **in the midst of the week** he shall cause the sacrifice and the oblation to cease, and for the overspreading of abominations he shall make *it* desolate, even until the consummation, and that determined shall be poured upon the desolate.

Now, what will happen on the earth during the **first 3 ½ years**?

As indicated above, during the *first 3 ½ years* of the seven-year tribulation, the nation of Israel will be at peace with the Anti-Christ, but the other nations will have to face the judgment of God. During that **first half** of the great tribulation, the inhabitants of the earth will be given one last opportunity to choose where they want to spend their eternity. The Church will not be on the earth at that time, because she was not included in the **70 weeks** that were determined upon the **children of Israel** and the **city of Jerusalem**.

The judgment of the **first 3 ½ years** will be executed in the following way:

① **The white horse:** *a false peace will be established on the earth*

② **The red horse:** *that false peace will be interrupted by chaos and discord*

③ **The black horse:** *food will be scarce and astronomically expensive*

④ **The pale horse:** *One fourth of the followers of the beast will be killed*

⑤ **The fifth seal:** *all of those who refuse the mark of the beast will be killed, and their souls will be taken to Heaven by the angels of God.*

- -

⑥ **The opening of the 6th seal:** ----- the events that are described in the revelation of the **sixth seal** do not concern the *first 3 ½ years* of the great tribulation. To understand what the revelation of the sixth seal is all about, you have to study it in parallel with the events that are described in the judgments of the **seven trumpets** and the **seven last plagues**.

Please take a look at the following comparisons:

Revelation 6:12-13 ---------➤ *Rev 8:5, 8:12, 9:2 / Acts 2:20, Joel 2:31*

The judgment of the **second 3 ½ years** will begin with a <u>**great**</u> earthquake (*Rev 8:5, 11:1-13*), but <u>at the end</u> of that **second 3 ½ years, the sun** and the **moon** will be darkened, and the stars will fall from heaven (Matt *24:29*)

Revelation 6:14 ---- ➤Isaiah *34:4, Hebrews 1:10-12, Revelation 20:11*

Revelation 6:15-17 --------➤ *Revelation 9:6, Isaiah 2:19, Luke 23:30*

Isaiah 2:19: "And they shall go into the holes of the rocks, and into the caves of the earth, for fear of the LORD, and for the glory of his majesty, when he ariseth to shake terribly the earth".

The judgments of the **seven trumpets** and the **seven last plagues** will not fall on the earth during the **first 3** $^{1/2}$ **years**. Those two judgments will be reserved specially for those who will accept the mark of the beast. (*Revelation 11:1-2*)

46

Revelation, chapter 7

The *first phase* of the judgment of the great tribulation is over, and now we are going to see the *second phase* of that judgment. In this seventh chapter, we are given three important pieces of information:

The **restraining** of the 4 angels who are positioned at the four corners of the earth (**Verse 1-3**)	*They will be released in* **chapter 9:13-15**
The **sealing** of the 144000 Jews from the **twelve tribes** of the Children of Israel (**Verse 4-8**)	*They will be mentioned once again in* **chapter 14:1-5**
The **gathering** of the martyrs who were slain on the earth for refusing the **mark** (**verse 9-17**)	*They will be mentioned once again in* **chapter 15:1-4**

What do those three pieces of information tell you about the seven-year tribulation? Do those two groups of people tell you something about the Church of Jesus-Christ? -- First of all, let's talk about the 144000 Jews:

Who are those *144000 Jews*? Do they really represent the Seventh Day Adventists? Do their seal really represents the Sabbath day? --- Here is a very clear and direct answer: those *144000 Jews* who were selected from the 12 tribes of the children of Israel have absolutely nothing to do with the *Seventh Day Adventists*, and their seal has nothing to do with the *Sabbath day either*. The seal that was placed on the foreheads of those *144000 Jews* is nothing else than the **name of God** (*Rev 14:2-3*).

Those 144000 Jews will not be sealed because they are Sabbath keepers, but rather they will only be sealed for their protection. They will not be allowed to be killed on the earth in the judgment of the **seven trumpets**. They will be sealed by the angels of God just like God had ordered his angels to set a **mark** upon the **foreheads** of the Jews who were **sighing** and **crying** for the abominations that were happening in the city of Jerusalem after the Babylonian exile. (*See Ezekiel 9:1-4*)

Now, let's talk about the great multitude. What did one of the 24 elders tell John concerning those people? Didn't he clearly reveal to John where they came from? Was he talking about the Church? Absolutely not! If those people really represented the glorified Church, they would not only have been accompanied by those who were saved before *the great tribulation*, but also they would have had the crown that was promised to the Church. In addition to that, they would not have appeared before God without their glorified bodies. (See *1 Thessalonians 4:13-17, 1 Corinthians 15:51-53*)

Now, here is what you need to understand about the revelation of the *144000 Jews* and the *great multitude that was slain on the earth*: first of all, remember that the seven-year tribulation will be divided into two equal parts of *42 months* (**3** $^{1/2}$ **years**). During the first **3** $^{1/2}$ **years**, the gentiles nations will be given one last opportunity to get saved. During that **first 3** $^{1/2}$ **years**, the Jews will not be obligated to take the mark of the beast because they will have already been engaged under a **seven-year peace agreement**. What will happen at the end of the first **3** $^{1/2}$ **years** of the great tribulation? Answer: the gentile nations will have been harvested.

48

No one on earth, except the Jews, will be able to survive throughout the **first 3 $^{1/2}$ years** without the mark of the beast. Every little thing that money can buy will be under the direct control of the enemy. Remember the **black horse** (*the famine*) of *Revelation 6:5-7.* Nobody will be authorized to **buy** or **sell** anything without the mark of the beast.

Now you can understand why that *great multitude* is gathered before the throne of God prior to the judgment of the **seven trumpets** and of the **seven last plagues.** The **second half** (*3 $^{1/2}$ years*) of the great tribulation will be a time of persecution for the Jews, and it will also be a time of severe punishment for those who will accept the mark of the beast during the **first 3 $^{1/2}$ years.** They will suffer the consequences of their choice.

Here are the three phases of the Judgment of the great tribulation:

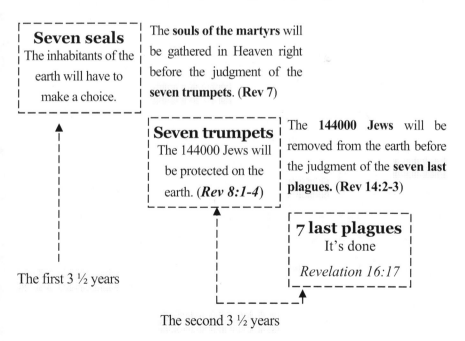

Seven seals
The inhabitants of the earth will have to make a choice.

The **souls of the martyrs** will be gathered in Heaven right before the judgment of the **seven trumpets**. (**Rev 7**)

Seven trumpets
The 144000 Jews will be protected on the earth. (***Rev 8:1-4***)

The **144000 Jews** will be removed from the earth before the judgment of the **seven last plagues.** (**Rev 14:2-3**)

7 last plagues
It's done

Revelation 16:17

The first 3 ½ years

The second 3 ½ years

Why have we said that the judgments of the seven trumpets and the seven last plagues will be executed during the second 3 $^{1/2}$ years?

The reason is very simple: if you turn you bible to *Revelation 11*, you will find two pieces of information that establish a clear difference between the *first* and the *second* **3 $^{1/2}$ years** of the great tribulation. Here is what is revealed in the first three verses of *Revelation 11*:

"11 And there was given me a reed like unto a rod: and the angel stood, saying, Rise, and measure **the temple of God**, and the altar, and them that worship therein. 2 But the court which is without the temple leave out, and measure it not; for it is given unto the **Gentiles**: and the holy city shall they tread under foot **forty and two months**. 3 And I will give power unto my **two witnesses**, and they shall prophesy **a thousand two hundred and threescore days**, clothed in sackcloth".

Have you seen the difference now? --- The **gentiles** will have **42 months** to set foot in the city of Jerusalem and the **two witnesses** of God will have **42 months** to prophesy in the land of Israel, but right after the death of the two witnesses, the events of **second 3 $^{1/2}$ years** will begin to be fulfilled. (*Rev 11*)

Now, here is what we are asking you to do: turn your bible to *Revelation 8:6-13* and read it very carefully. When you are finished reading that passage, try to reflect on these questions for a few minutes: Will the **two witnesses** be able to fulfill their **42 months** of ministry under the terrible judgment of the **seven trumpets**? Will the **gentiles** be able to travel back and forth to the city of Jerusalem, for **42 months**, under such a terrible judgment? --- No, It will not be possible. God will not disturb the ministry of the two witnesses. He will not send the judgment of the **7 trumpets** during the **first 3 $^{1/2}$ years**. It's for no reason that the *144000* Jews are protected from that judgment.

Revelation, chapters 8-9-10
The suffering of the followers of the Anti-Christ

Right now, we are in the judgment of the seven trumpets. All you have to do now is read those three chapters very carefully without forgetting to pay attention to the difference between the **first** and the **second 3 ½ years**.

As we said before, the **second 3 ½ years** of the great tribulation is strictly reserved for the fulfillment of the prophecy of **Daniel 7:23-25** (*the persecution of the nation of Israel*) and for the punishment of those who took the mark of the beast during the **first 3 ½ years**.

Note: the **eagle** that is mentioned in **chapter 8** should not be taken literally, because we all know that an **eagle** can't speak. The **star** that is mentioned in *chapter 9: 1-12* is also an **angel** of God, and the **locusts** that are coming out of the bottomless pit are clearly described in the same chapter. All of those things were shown to the Apostle John from a distance. The focus of the Revelation of the Lord Jesus was placed exclusively on his message.

Here is another simple way you can tell the difference between the **first** and the **second 3 ½ years** : in the judgment of the **seven seals**, the **demons of hell** were released on the earth, and they were given the order to kill **ONE-FOURTH** of the population who had the mark of the beast (*Rev 6:8*). But now, in the judgment of the **seven trumpets**, the **demons of hell** are ordered to kill **ONE-THIRD** of those who have the mark (*Rev 9:13-21*). Each one of those two groups of people will be killed respectively during the **first** and the **second 3 ½ years** of the great tribulation. (*Very important!*)

Revelation, chapters 11-12-13

The focus of the book of Revelation is now placed on the nation of Israel and the Anti-Christ.

Just before we get into the study of those three chapters, let us first of all take a look at the following illustration:

This is the judgment of the **seven seals:**

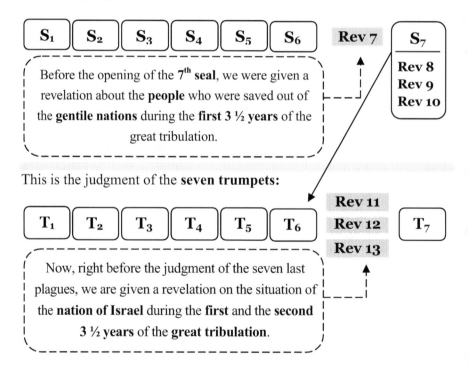

This is the judgment of the **seven trumpets:**

Now in order to begin with the study of those three chapters, the first thing we're going to have to do is harmonize the details of the eleventh chapter with the prophetic timeline of **Daniel 9:27** (*the 70th week*).

Revelation, chapter 11

The mission of the two witnesses of God in the land of Israel

Daniel 9: 27:

"And he shall confirm the covenant with many for **one week**" (**seven years**)

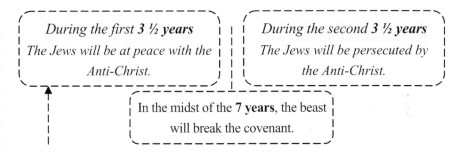

According to the details of the eleventh chapter of the book of Revelation, during the **first 3 ½ years** of the great tribulation:

- There will be a **temple in Jerusalem**
- The **Mosaic law** will be reinstated *(Daniel 7:23-25, 9:27, 12:11)*
- The gentiles will be allowed to set foot in Jerusalem for **42 months**
- God will send his **two witnesses** in the Land of Israel to confront the **rulers** of the people for a period of **1260 days (42 months)**

|| 1260 days ÷ 30 days = **42 months (or 3 ½ years)** ||

When the *42 months* of the **two witnesses** are over, the Anti-Christ will kill them (*Rev 11:7*), and right after that, the Anti-Christ will be allowed to continue for another *42 months* (*Rev 13:1-5*).

To understand the message of those three chapters that we are studying now, you need to pay attention to the frequent repetition of the *number of days.*

The revelation of the Ark of the Covenant of God

Rev 11:19: *"and the temple of God was opened in heaven, and there was seen in his temple the **ark of his testament**: and there were lightnings, and voices, and thunderings, and an earthquake, and great hail"*.

The children of Israel are not abandoned by God. The promise of the **New Covenant** that was made to them in *Jeremiah 31:31-32*, will be fulfilled at the second coming of the Lord Jesus.

 ← **The Ark of the Old Covenant** that was placed in the holy of holies was a shadow of the **Ark of the New Covenant** that is mentioned above.

Jeremiah 31: 31-32:

"31 Behold, the days come, saith the Lord, that **I will make a new covenant** with the **house of Israel**, and with the house of **Judah**: 32 **not according to the covenant** that I made with their fathers in the day that I took them by the hand to bring them out of the land of Egypt; which my **covenant they brake**, although I was an **husband** unto them, saith the Lord":

The gentiles will be allowed to set foot in the city of God (*Jerusalem*) for a period of **42 months** (*3 $^{1/2}$ years*), but during the **second 42 months** of the seven-year tribulation, the heathens will not be allowed to access the city.

The **Ark of the Testimony** of God was not revealed in the book of Revelation without any reason. This is a very clear message that God is sending to us concerning the children of Israel, because he does not want us to be ignorant about his purpose for the children of Israel.

Revelation, chapter 12

The woman and the great red dragon in the second heaven

The revelation of this 12th chapter is divided into three parts:

Revelation 12:1-6

1. The woman and her child
2. The great red dragon and the third of the stars
3. The protection of the woman in the wilderness for a
   ▶ period of **1260 days** (3 ½ years or 42 months)

Revelation 12:7-12

1. The **war in the second heaven**
2. the casting out of Satan and his angels from the second heaven.
3. The great wrath of the dragon against the woman

Revelation 12:13-17

1. The persecution the woman
2. The protection of God in favor of the woman
3. The dragon launches his attacks against the **remnant** of the woman. And the woman is protected for **a time,** ▶**times**, and **a dividing of time.** (*Daniel 7: 23-27*)

First 3 ½ years ‖	(Second 3 ½ years)	‖ Second 3 ½ years
Rev 11: 1260 days	**Rev 12**: 1260 days	**Rev 13**: the Anti-Christ will continue for another 42 months.
Rev 11: 42 months	A time, times, a dividing of time.	

Here is a very simple way the vision of chapter 12 can be interpreted:

First of all, let's take a look at the details that are provided about the **woman**

- *She was clothed with the **sun***
- *The **moon** was under her feet*
- *She had a crown of **twelve stars** upon her head*

Now, the second passage we are going to read in parallel with the details that are listed above is found in *Genesis 37:9-11.*

"9 and <u>he</u> dreamed yet another dream, and told it his brethren, and said, Behold, I have dreamed a dream more; and, behold, the **sun** and the **moon** and the **eleven stars** made obeisance to me. 10 And he told it to his father and to his brethren":

Joseph didn't understand the dream, but his father Jacob did.

Verse 10-11: "And **his father rebuked him**, and said unto him, what is this dream that thou hast dreamed? Shall **I** and thy **mother** and **thy brethren** indeed come to *bow down* ourselves to thee to the earth? 11 And his brethren envied him; but his father observed the saying".

Note: the reason why Joseph saw only **11 stars** in the dream that he had, it's simply because he was not included among those *11 stars*. But he was also one of the 12 sons of Jacob.

Now, here is what you need to understand: the same God who gave the prophetic dream of *Genesis 37* to Joseph, also gave the vision of *Revelation 12* to the Apostle John. The message that God is communicating to his Church through the symbolic images of the **sun**, the **moon**, and the **12 stars** is clearly explained in the passage of Genesis 37:10-11. All of those three symbolic images remind us of one thing: the **origin** of the nation of Israel.

Why is the nation of Israel represented by a **woman**?

The reason why the nation of Israel is represented by a **woman**, it's simply because of the **covenant** that she had contracted with God on **Mount Sinai**.

Israel was in a covenant relationship with God:
(Isaiah 54:4-6, 8-10)

"4 Fear not; for thou shalt not be ashamed: neither be thou confounded; for thou shalt not be put to shame: for thou shalt forget the shame of thy youth, and shalt not remember the reproach of thy **widowhood** any more.

For thy Maker *is* thine **husband**; the LORD of hosts *is* his name; and thy Redeemer the Holy One of Israel; The God of the whole earth shall he be called. ⁶ For the LORD hath called thee **as a woman forsaken** and grieved in spirit, and a **wife** of youth, when thou wast refused, saith thy God".

7 For a small moment have **I forsaken thee**; but with great mercies will I gather thee. 8 In a little wrath I hid my face from thee for a moment; but with everlasting kindness will I have mercy on thee, saith the LORD thy Redeemer

----

The male Child of the woman

Verses 4-5: "… and the **dragon** stood before the woman which was ready to be delivered, for *to devour her child as soon as it was born.* "And **she** brought forth a man child, who was to **rule all nations** with a rod of iron: and her child was caught up unto God and to his throne";

The **nation of Israel** represents the **woman** who brought forth the **male child** (Jesus-Christ) who will *rule all the nations with a rod of iron.*

Revelation 19:15: "15 And out of his mouth goeth a sharp sword, that with it he should **smite the nations**: and he shall rule them with a rod of iron: and he treadeth the winepress of the fierceness and wrath of Almighty God".

Satan hates the 12th chapter of the book of Revelation. It is obviously not a coincidence if so many people have so much difficulty agreeing on the identity of the **woman**. The lack of spiritual discernment can cause people to fall easily into the trap of confusion of the enemy. The idea of saying that the **woman** is symbol of the Church is completely erroneous. The Church did not bring forth the Son of God, but rather, it was the Lord Jesus who built the Church after his ascension to Heaven.

The failed assassination attempt of Satan against the Son of God

"3 And there appeared another wonder in heaven; and behold **a great red dragon**, having **seven heads** and **ten horns**, and **seven crowns** upon his heads. 4 And his tail drew the **third part of the stars of heaven**, and did cast them to the earth: and the dragon stood before the woman which was ready to be delivered, for to devour her child as soon as it was born".

We all know the story of the massacre that was perpetrated by King Herod in the land of Bethlehem after the Lord Jesus was born, and we also know that the **Roman Empire** is included among the **seven heads** (*kingdoms*) of the great red dragon that is described in the above passage. Now, based on those two facts, it is quite self-evident that Satan was the mastermind behind that massacre; he was angry at the deliverance of the **woman** (*Israel*).

The expulsion of Satan from the second heaven

Verses 7-9: "**7** And there was war **in heaven**: Michael and his angels fought against the dragon; and the dragon fought and his angels, **8** and prevailed not; neither was **their place found** any more **in heaven.**

"And the great dragon was cast out, that old **serpent**, called the **Devil**, and **Satan**, which deceiveth the whole world: **he was cast out into the earth**, and **his angels** were cast out with him".

Where did the Apostle John see that war? Was it in the **second heaven** or was it in the **third heaven**? *Answer*: the Apostle John was not talking about the **third Heaven**, as many people believe. To understand which heaven the Apostle John was actually talking about, you have to read those two verses that are quoted above in the general context of the 12th chapter.

Here is what you need to pay attention to:

Rev 12: 1: "And there appeared a great wonder **in heaven**; a woman clothed with the sun, and the moon under her feet, and upon her head a crown of twelve stars: "

Rev 12: 3: " And there appeared another wonder **in heaven**; and behold a great red dragon, having seven heads and ten horns, and seven crowns upon his heads "

Did the Apostle John see those images in the **third Heaven**? Absolutely not! The great red dragon did not leave the **second heaven** to go make war in the **third Heaven**, but it was exactly the opposite that happened. The idea of saying that Satan will go to the third Heaven to lead another rebellion among the **elect angels** is a very dangerous teaching. There will be no such event in the house of God during the seven-year tribulation. Just

59

because it is said that "neither was **their place** found any more **in heaven**" does not mean that the Apostle John was talking about the angels who dwell in the **third Heaven**. The angels who followed Satan in his rebellion against God are clearly mentioned in the fourth verse of the 12th chapter:

"3 And there appeared another wonder in heaven; and behold a great red dragon, having seven heads and ten horns, and seven crowns upon his heads. 4 And **his tail** drew **the third part of the stars of heaven**, and did **cast them to the earth**"

There will be no more rebellion among the elect angels who are mentioned in *Revelation 5:11*. We should not believe something that is not in the bible. The revelation of God is very clear: Satan will be **expelled** from the **second heaven** because the seven-year tribulation will mark the end of his reign.

Revelation 12: "10 And I heard a loud voice saying in heaven, Now is come salvation, and strength, and the kingdom of our God, and the power of his Christ: for the accuser of our brethren is **cast down**, which accused them before our God day and night. **11** And they overcame him by the blood of the Lamb, and by the word of their testimony; and they loved not their lives unto the death".

"**12** therefore rejoice ye heavens, and ye that dwell in them. Woe to the inhabiters of the earth and of the sea! For the **devil** is *come down unto you*, **having great wrath**, because he knoweth that he hath but **a short time**".

Those wicked spirits who dwell in the heavenly realms *(Ephesians 6:12)* are persecuting the Church, but when they are cast down unto the earth during the seven-year tribulation, they will not find the Church on the earth, because the **bride of Christ** will have already been removed from the earth.

The last attack of Satan against the woman (Israel)

Verses 13-14: "And when the dragon saw that he was **cast unto the earth**, he persecuted the *woman* which brought forth the **man child**. [14] And to the **woman** were given **two wings of a great eagle** that she might fly into the wilderness, into her place, where she is nourished for **a time**, and **times**, and **half a time**, from the face of the serpent".

The "**two wings of a great eagle**" is a spiritual expression that makes reference to God's protection in favor of the nation of Israel.

How will God protect the nation of Israel during the great tribulation?

Daniel 12:1:
"And **at that time** shall Michael stand up, the great prince which standeth **for the children of thy people**: and **there shall be a time of trouble, such as never was** *since there was a nation even to that same time*: and at that time thy **people** shall be delivered, every one that shall be found written in the book.

this prophecy makes a clear reference to the period of the great tribulation.

How will Satan attack the children of Israel?

verses 15-17: "And the serpent cast out of his mouth **water as a flood** after the woman, that he might cause her to be **carried away of the flood**. 16 And the **earth helped the woman**, and the earth opened her mouth, and swallowed up the flood which the dragon cast out of his mouth". (**See Zachariah 14:1-5**)

He will make an attempt to annihilate the entire nation of Israel by way of the other nations (*the waters*), but God will his people throughout the earth.

61

The enemy will gather the armies of the nations to attack the nation of Israel, but his annihilation attempt will be aborted. At the second coming of the Lord Jesus, the nations of the earth will be judged because of the Children of Israel. (*See Matthew 25:31-46*)

Who will Satan attack specifically among the children of Israel?

"**¹⁷** and the dragon was wroth with the woman, and went to make war with the **remnant** of her seed, which *keep the commandments of God*, and *have the testimony of Jesus Christ*".

> He will attack those who will see the judgment of the great tribulation.
>
> **Romans 9:27**: "Isaiah also crieth concerning Israel, Though the number of the children of Israel be as the **sand of the sea**, a **remnant** shall be saved". (Isaiah 1:9, 10:20-22)

The **remnant** that Satan will attempt to annihilate during the **second 3 ½ years** of the great tribulation represents all of those who will open their hearts to the message that God will send to the nation of Israel by the way of the **two witnesses** (*Revelation 11*) and the **144000 Jews** (*Revelation 7, 9*).

The **remnant** that is mentioned in Revelation 12 has absolutely nothing to do with the **Seventh-day Adventist Church**. The Church of God was built once and for all on the day of Pentecost, and it was never rebuilt in 1844.

During the **seven-year tribulation**, all the Jews will have a golden opportunity to get saved, but not all of them will respond to God's calling.

Romans 11:1-5:

"[11] I say then, Hath God **cast away** his people? God forbid. For I also am an **Israelite**, of the seed of Abraham, of the tribe of Benjamin. 2 God hath not cast away his people which he foreknew. Wot ye not what the scripture saith of Elias? how he maketh intercession to God against **Israel**, saying, 3 Lord, they have killed thy prophets, and digged down thine altars; and I am left alone, and they seek my life. 4 But what saith the answer of God unto him? I have reserved to myself seven thousand men, who have not bowed the knee to the image of Baal.

"5 Even so then at this **present time** also there is a **remnant** according to the election of grace."

The promise of God toward the nation of Israel will not change

Romans 11:25-28:

"[25] For I would not, brethren, that ye should be ignorant of **this mystery**, lest ye should be wise in your own conceits; that blindness in part is happened to **Israel**, until the **fullness of the Gentiles** be come in. 26 And so **all Israel shall be saved**: as it is written, There shall come out of Sion the Deliverer, and shall turn away ungodliness from **Jacob**: 27 for this is my **covenant** unto them, when I shall take away their sins. 28 As concerning the gospel, they are enemies for your sakes: but as touching the election, they are beloved for the fathers' sakes.

The people of the Old Covenant is not forgotten by their God. The enemy is trying to replace the **remnant** of children of Israel by a **man-made remnant**, but the word of God is powerful enough to lead us into the whole truth. There will not be a remnant Church which will be attacked by Satan during the great tribulation. The Church of God will be in Heaven with the Lord Jesus.

63

The duration of the persecution of the woman

The last point that we are going to address in the present section is going to be based on a parallel between *verses 6* and *14*. What you are going to see from this comparison will be self-evident enough to prove to you that the **woman** of Revelation 12 is indeed a symbolic picture of the nation of Israel.

Here is what is said in verse 6:

"5 And she brought forth a man child, who was to rule all nations with a rod of iron: and her child was caught up unto God, and to his throne. 6 And the woman fled into the **wilderness**, where she hath a place prepared of God, that they should feed her there a **thousand two hundred** and **threescore days**". (**1260 days**)

Here is what is said in verse 14:

13 And when the dragon saw that he was cast unto the earth, he persecuted the woman which brought forth the man child. 14 And to the **woman** were given two wings of a great eagle, that she might fly into the **wilderness**, into her place, where she is nourished for **a time**, and **times**, and **half a time**, from the face of the serpent. (**3 $^{1/2}$ years**)

Now, would you like to understand why the duration of the persecution of the woman is repeated twice and in two different ways? --- Here is a very simple way you can find out why the revelation was given in that way:

First of all, you need to turn back to the passage of *Revelation 11: 1-7* so that you can compare the **1260 days** of the *two witnesses* with the **1260 days** of the *woman*. Secondly, you need to turn back to the prophecy of *Daniel 7:23-25* in order to compare it with the passage of *Revelation 12:14*.

Please take a look at this first comparison:

Revelation 11	Revelation 12
3 And I will give power unto my **two witnesses**, and they shall prophesy a *thousand two hundred and threescore days*, clothed in sackcloth. (**1260 days**) **1260 days** ÷ *30 = 42 months*	6 And the woman fled into the **wilderness**, where she hath a place prepared of God, that they should feed her there a *thousand two hundred* and *threescore* **days**". **1260 days** ÷ *30 = 42 months*

Let us now take a look once again at the prophecy of Daniel 9:27:

Daniel 9: 27:

"And he shall confirm the covenant with many for **one week**" (**seven years**)

During the first 3 ½ years *The Jews will be at peace with the* *Anti-Christ for 42 months.*	*During the second 3 ½ years* *The Jews will be persecuted by* *the Anti-Christ for 42 months.*

In the midst of the **7 years**, the beast will break the covenant.

The two witnesses of God will prophesy for **3** $^{1/2}$ **years** (*42 months*), and at the end of their ministry, they will be killed by the Anti-Christ (*Rev 11:7*). After the Anti-Christ will have killed the two witnesses, he will be allowed to continue for another **42 months** (**3** $^{1/2}$ **years**). Now remember: Israel will not be persecuted during the first **3** $^{1/2}$ **years** of the great tribulation, but rather, her persecution will begin right after the killing of the two witnesses. That's exactly what God is revealing to us through the *1260 days* of Revelation 12.

65

The **1260 days** that are mentioned in *Revelation 12:6* make reference to the second **3** $^{1/2}$ **years** of the great tribulation; *the time of Jacob's trouble,* and the **3** $^{1/2}$ **years** that are mentioned in *Revelation 12:14* also makes reference to the prophecy that was given in Daniel 7:23-25.

In Rev 12:6 we read the following:

"5 And she brought forth a man child, who was to rule all nations with a rod of iron: and her child was caught up unto God, and to his throne. 6 And the woman fled into the **wilderness**, where she hath a place prepared of God, that they should feed her there a **thousand two hundred** and **threescore days**". (**1260 days**)

In Rev 12:14 we read the following:

13 And when the dragon saw that he was cast unto the earth, he persecuted the woman which brought forth the man child. 14 And to the **woman** were given two wings of a great eagle, that she might fly into the **wilderness**, into her place, where she is nourished for **a time**, and **times**, and **half a time**, from the face of the serpent. (*3* $^{1/2}$ *years, 42 months, or 1260 days*)

Here is what God had revealed to Daniel concerning the persecution of the against of the Anti-Christ against the children of Israel during the seven-year tribulation:

24 And the **ten horns** out of this kingdom are **ten kings** that shall arise: and **another** shall rise after them; and **he** shall be diverse from the first, and he shall subdue **three kings**. 25 And he shall **speak great words** against the most High, and shall wear out **the saints** of the most High, and think to change **times** and **laws**: and they shall be given into his hand until **a time** and **times** and the **dividing of time**. (*Daniel 7:23-25*) (*See also Revelation 17:12*)

What else can we say about the identity of the **woman**? The word of God is true; it's pure; it's clear; it's accurate, and above all, it's self-explanatory.

Revelation, Chapter 13

The appearing and the reappearing of the Anti-Christ on the world stage

---

Revelation 13: 1: "And I stood upon the sand of the sea, and saw a **beast** *rise up out of the sea*, having **seven heads** and **ten horns**, and upon his horns **ten crowns**, and upon his heads the name of blasphemy.

Here is how the kingdom of the beast is described in the book of Daniel:

Daniel 7: 7-8: "[7] After this I saw in the night visions, and behold **a fourth beast**, *dreadful* and *terrible*, and *strong exceedingly*; and it had great *iron teeth*: it devoured and brake in pieces, and stamped the **residue** with the feet of it: and it was diverse from all the beasts that were before it; and it had **ten horns**. 8 *I considered* **the horns**, and, behold, *there came up among them* **another little horn**, before whom there were three of the first horns plucked up by the roots: and, behold, in **this horn** were eyes like the eyes of man, and a *mouth speaking great things*"

The same words are once again repeated in the book of Revelation:

Revelation 13: 5: "and there was given unto him *a mouth speaking great things* and **blasphemies**; and power was given unto him **to continue forty and two months**". 6 And he opened his mouth in blasphemy against God, to blaspheme his name, and **his tabernacle**, and them that dwell in heaven".

Please note: the *1260 day-prophecy* that we just studied in the **12th chapter** will be fulfilled exactly during the *42 months* which will be granted to the Anti-Christ. The dragon will attack Israel during the **second 3 $^{1/2}$ years**.

The characteristics of the last world kingdom

Verse 2: "And the **beast** which I saw was like unto a **leopard**, and his **feet** were as the **feet of a bear**, and his mouth as the **mouth of a lion**: and the **dragon** gave him his power, and his seat, and great authority".

The last world kingdom which will be established on the earth will possess the characteristics of the three world Empires that followed the Babylonian Empire (*Daniel 7:1-8*). It will devour the whole earth like a **ferocious** *lion*; it will trample the nations like a *angry bear* **tramples** its prey, and it will be **swift** in its acts of wickedness in like manner as a *leopard*. That's why it'll be different from all the other kingdoms.

Daniel 7:7
7 After this I saw in the night visions, and behold a **fourth beast, dreadful** and **terrible**, and **strong exceedingly**; and it had **great iron teeth**: it **devoured** and **brake in pieces**, and stamped the residue **with the feet** of it: and it was **diverse** from all the beasts that were before it; and it had **ten horns**.

Rev 13: 3-5: "3 And I saw one of his heads as it were *wounded to death*; and his **deadly wound was healed**: and all the world wondered after the beast.

That event will mark the end of the **1260 days** of the two witnesses or the end of the **first 3 $^{1/2}$ years** of the seven-year tribulation.

Revelation 11:7: "7 And when they shall have **finished their testimony**, the beast that ascendeth **out of the bottomless pit** shall make war against them, and shall overcome them, and kill them".

The Appearing of the second beast (**Verses 11-18**)

This **second beast** that will stand by the side of the Anti-Christ during the seven-year tribulation is clearly identified as a **false prophet** in *Revelation 16:13, 19:20, 20:10,* and his **religious organization** (BABYLON THE GREAT) is also revealed in *Revelation 17-18.* When the word of God says that the *second beast* had two horns like a **lamb**, and spake like a dragon, that's a typical picture of a religious leader. The message can't be any clearer than that. Now, in regards to the question pertaining to the identity of the Anti-Christ, we don't really have anything to say about that, because the word of God is already clear on that point: the identity of the Anti-Christ will not be revealed before the appointed time.

Please take a look at the following verses:

2 Thessalonians 2:3-4: "³ Let no man **deceive** you by any means: for that day shall not come, except there come a falling away first, and *that man of sin be revealed*, the **son of perdition**". (*Verse 4........*)

"5 Remember ye not, that, when I was yet with you, I told you these things? 6 And now ye know what **withholdeth** that he might be **revealed in his time**. 7 For **the mystery of iniquity** doth already work: only he who now letteth will let, until he be taken out of the way".

The candidates for the offices of the **Anti-Christ** and the **false prophet** have been around since the time of the early Church (*1 Jean 2:18*), because the day of the Rapture has always been a mystery to the enemy. Nobody really knows for sure who the false prophet is, but we can all agree that it is **he** who will be the last leader of the **Harlot Church** of Babylon (*Rev 17-18*).

69

Revelation, chapter 14 and 15:1-2

The message that is contained in this *14th chapter* is divided into four points:

1. The glorification of the 144000 Jews *(Verses 1-5)*
2. The messages of the three angels *(Verses 6-12)*
3. The words of blessing of the angel to the Church *(Verse 13)*
4. The final harvest of the earth *(Verses 14-20)*

The glorification of the 144000 Jews

> **Revelation 14**: 1: "and I looked, and, lo, a Lamb stood on the mount Sion, and
> with him an **hundred forty and four thousand**, having his **Father's name**
> written in their *foreheads*".

The *144000 Jews* who were sealed in *chapter 7* are now in Heaven. Contrary to the **great multitude** that was slain on the earth, those *144000 Jews* will not be allowed to be killed on the earth, but they will all be taken up to Heaven without tasting death. This special group of people are not members of the body of Christ, but they will be chosen as **firstfruits** among those who will be saved during the seven-year tribulation.

It is extremely important to understand the difference between the **Church,** the **144000 Jews**, and the **great multitude**. Each one of those three groups of redeemed are totally separated from one another. Those who will be killed on the earth during the **first 3 ½ years** *(the great multitude)* will be reunited with their physical bodies at the second coming of the Lord Jesus.

Please take a careful look at the following passages:

The great multitude *of Revelation 7:9-17*

[9] After this I beheld, and, lo, a **great multitude**, which no man could number, of all nations, and kindreds, and people, and tongues, stood before the throne, and before the Lamb, clothed with white robes, and palms in their hands;

Verse 14: ….These are they which came **out of great tribulation……**

The great multitude *in Revelation15:1-2*

15 And I saw another sign in heaven, great and marvellous, seven angels having the seven last plagues; for in them is filled up the wrath of God. [2] And I saw as it were a sea of glass mingled with fire: and <u>them</u> that had gotten the victory over the **beast**, and over his **image**, and over his **mark**, *and* over the **number of his name**, stand on the sea of glass, having the harps of God.

The great multitude *in Revelation 20:4-5* ❸

[4] And I saw thrones, and they sat upon them, and judgment was given unto them: and *I saw* the **souls** of **them** that <u>were</u> **beheaded** for the witness of Jesus, and for the word of God, and which had not **worshipped** the **beast**, neither his **image**, neither had received *his* **mark** upon their foreheads, or in their hands; and <u>they lived</u> and reigned with Christ a thousand years.
(See Revelation 6:9-11)
5 But **the rest of the dead** *lived not again* until the thousand years were finished.

Please note: the gentiles who will be saved during the great tribulation will not be divided into two groups. All of those people will be taken up to Heaven *in the spirit*, and they will all stand before God as one group. *(Revelation 6:9-11)*

71

If it is true that the Church of Jesus-Christ will be on the earth during the **seven-year tribulation**, then why are the **144000 Jews** called the **first fruits** of God and of the Lamb? Does not the bible say in **James 1:18** that the Church is the **first fruits** of God's creatures? Will God change his promise toward the Church that was built in the land of Israel? Absolutely not!

Here is how the Lord Jesus sees his Church

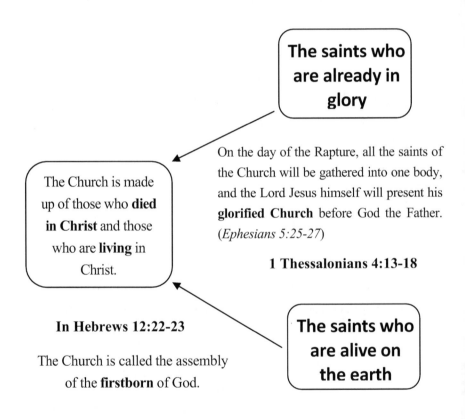

The saints who are already in glory

On the day of the Rapture, all the saints of the Church will be gathered into one body, and the Lord Jesus himself will present his **glorified Church** before God the Father. (*Ephesians 5:25-27*)

The Church is made up of those who **died in Christ** and those who are **living** in Christ.

1 Thessalonians 4:13-18

In Hebrews 12:22-23

The Church is called the assembly of the **firstborn** of God.

The saints who are alive on the earth

The Assembly of the **first born of God** is made up of **Jews** and **gentiles** who are united into one body with Christ under the *dispensation of the Holy Spirit*. The Church of Jesus-Christ is unique and indivisible.

Let's now take a look at the difference between the *song* of the **144000 Jews** and the song of the **great multitude**:

The song of the 144000 Jews

"1 And I looked, and, lo, a Lamb stood on the mount **Sion**, and with him an **hundred forty and four thousand**, having his **Father's name** written in their foreheads. 2 And I heard a voice from heaven, as the voice of many waters, and as the voice of a great thunder: and I heard the voice of harpers harping with their harps: 3 and they sung as it were **a new song** before the throne, and before the four beasts, and the elders: and no man could **learn** that song but the hundred and forty and four thousand, which were redeemed from the earth.

The song of the great multitude

"1 And I saw another sign in heaven, great and marvelous, seven angels having the **seven last plagues**; for in them is filled up the wrath of God. 2 And I saw as it were a sea of glass mingled with fire: and **them** that had gotten the victory over the **beast**, and over his **image**, and over his **mark**, and over the **number** of **his name**, stand on the sea of glass, having the harps of God. 3 And they sing **the song of Moses** the servant of God, and **the song of the Lamb**, saying, Great and marvelous are thy works, Lord God Almighty; just and true are thy ways, thou King of saints".

As you can see from the above comparison, the song of the **144000 Jews** and the song of the **great multitude** are totally different. The **great multitude** was not sealed on the earth like the *144000 Jews*, they were not removed from the earth in the same way as the *144000 Jews*, and above all they are not accompanied by the saints who died before the seven-year tribulation. The **great multitude** that was slain on the earth does not represent the Church.

② The messages of the three angels *(Rev 14:6-11)*

"6 And I saw another **angel** fly in the midst of heaven, having the everlasting gospel to **preach** unto them *that dwell on the earth*, and to **every nation**, and **kindred**, and **tongue**, and **people**, 7 saying with a loud voice, Fear God, and give glory to him; **for the hour of his judgment is come**: and worship him that made heaven, and earth, and the sea, and the fountains of waters".

The judgment of the city of the false prophet

"8 And there followed another **angel**, saying, Babylon is **fallen**, is **fallen**, **that great city**, because she made all nations drink of the wine of the wrath of her fornication. *(See Revelation 17-18)*

9 And the *third* **angel** followed them, saying with a loud voice, If any man worship the **beast** and his **image**, and receive his **mark** in his forehead, or in his hand, 10 the same shall drink of the wine of the wrath of God, which is poured out without mixture into the cup of his indignation; and he shall be tormented with fire and brimstone in the presence of the holy angels, and in the presence of the Lamb: *(Revelation 13:15-18)*

The good news of the *gospel of grace* which was rejected by the world will no longer be preached in the world during the seven year-tribulation. The eternal gospel of the **first angel** will be clear and simple: " .... *Fear God, and give glory to him; for the hour of his judgment is come"*.

The seven-year tribulation will be a time of **judgment** for the world. The Church of God will not be included in that judgment, because she is already covered by the blood of the Lamb. The eternal gospel which will

74

be preached to the inhabitants of the earth was also preached to the disciples of the Lord Jesus in the following terms: " *28 and fear not them which kill the body, but are not able to kill the soul: but rather fear him which is able to destroy both **soul** and **body** in hell*". (*Matthew 10:28*)

The fear of God is something that will remain engraved in the hearts of the creatures of God for all eternity, because it is the only thing that can spare the sinner from the judgment of God. The world does not have the fear of God. So, that's why God will send them that eternal gospel through an angel. All of those who reject that opportunity will have no excuse before God.

The blessing of the Church

Verse 13: "And I heard a voice from heaven saying unto me, Write, Blessed are the dead which die in the Lord from henceforth: Yea, saith the Spirit, that they may rest from their labours; and their works do follow them".

In the book of Revelation, there are **six** different blessing that are addressed exclusively to the members of the body of Christ (*Rev 14:13, 16:15, 19:9, 20:6, 22:7, and 22:14*). Those words of blessing do not concern the martyrs of the great tribulation, because they are not members of the Church.

Here is another example:
Revelation 16: 15: "Behold, I come as a **thief**. **Blessed** is he that watcheth, and keepeth his garments, lest he walk naked, and they see his shame".

Will that warning apply to those who will hear the messages of the three angels during the great tribulation? Is the Lord Jesus talking to those who will be killed for refusing the mark of the beast? Absolutely not!

75

④ The final harvest of the earth *(Rev 14:14-20)*

The person with the crown is the Lord Jesus

"14 And I looked, and behold a white cloud, and upon the cloud one sat like unto **the Son of man**, having on his head **a golden crown**, and in his hand a sharp sickle. 15 And another angel came out of the temple, crying with a loud voice to him that sat on the cloud, Thrust in thy sickle, and reap: for the time is come for thee to reap; for the harvest of the earth is ripe. 16 And he that sat on the cloud thrust in his sickle on the earth; and the earth was **reaped**".

The interpretation of the above passage can be found in *Matthew 13:25-40*:

"37 He answered and said unto them, **He** that soweth **the good seed** is **the Son of man**; 38 The field is the world; the good seed are the children of the kingdom; but the **tares** are the children of the wicked one; 39 The enemy that sowed them is the devil; the **harvest** is the **end of the world**; and the **reapers** are the **angels**".
He that soweth the **good seed** is the **Son of man** (See R*ev 14:14-16*)
And the **reapers** are the angels (See *Rev14:17-19*).

The period of the seven-year tribulation will be a time of harvest. All of the nations of the earth, including the nation of Israel, will be harvested. The children of the kingdom will include: the **Church**, the **great multitude**, the **144000 Jews**, the **faithful remnant** of the children of Israel, as well as those who will be saved during the judgment of the nations (*Matt 25:31-46*). For the time being, we are in the harvest of the first fruits (*the Church*), but the time of the **final harvest** (*the end of the world*) will be triggered by the **Rapture of the Church** (*the day of the gathering of the first fruits*).

76

Please take a look at the following passage:

Luke 10:1-2: "After these things the Lord appointed other seventy also, and sent them two and two before his face into every city and place, whither he himself would come. 2 Therefore said he unto them, The **harvest** *truly is great*, but the labourers are few: pray ye therefore the Lord of the **harvest**, that he would send forth labourers into his **harvest**".

The angels of God will reap the tears

Revelation 14: 17: "And another angel came out of the temple which is in heaven, he also having a sharp sickle. 18 And another angel came out from the altar, which had power over fire; and cried with a loud cry to him that had the sharp sickle, saying, Thrust in thy sharp sickle, and gather the clusters of the vine of the earth; for her grapes are fully ripe. 19 And the angel thrust in his sickle into the earth, and gathered the vine of the earth, and cast it into the great winepress of **the wrath of God**.

At the second coming of the Lord Jesus, the angels of God will cast the enemies of Israel into the lake of fire.

Revelation, chapter 15

The seven last plagues

So far, everything is clear. The **seven last plagues** (*or the third woe*) will complete the judgment of the great tribulation. Those who have the mark will suffer all these things that are described in the following chapter.

Revelation, chapter 16

----

1. A noisome and grievous sore is poured on those who have the mark
2. The sea turns into blood
3. The rivers and the water fountains turn into blood
4. Those who have the mark are burnt by the heat of the sun
5. The kingdom of the beast is covered with darkness
6. The Euphrates rivers is dried up
7. A great earthquake splits the **great city** of the false prophet (**Babylon**).

Revelation 16:17:

And the Apostle John heard the voice of the Lord Jesus from heaven saying:

"It is finished".

End of the great tribulation

Revelation, chapters 17-18

Mystery, Babylon the great, the mother of **harlots** and abominations of the earth

----

The message of the seventeenth chapter of the book of Revelation is a **coded message** through which God is warning his Church against a corrupt religious system that has authority over the **kings** and the **inhabitants** of the earth. In the details that are provided by the angel, we are said that the **whore of Babylon** is a **rich city**. That place of spiritual prostitution is also identified as the meeting place for the **wicked** and the **unclean spirits** of the air (*Rev 18:1-3*), and above all, we are said that she's guilty of the blood of the **Apostles**, the **prophets**, and the **saints** of the Lord Jesus (*Rev 18:23-24*).

Although the city of Babylon is not identified by name, but the details that are provided about her are more than enough to help us understand that the whore of Babylon is none other than the **False Church** that worships the **queen of the second heaven**. "*All roads lead to Rome*".

Does God want his people to unite themselves with the whore of Babylon?

"4 And I heard another voice from heaven, saying, Come out of her, my people, that ye be not partakers of her sins, and that ye receive not of her plagues. 5 For her sins have reached unto heaven, and God hath remembered her iniquities".

God will not spare any of those who are involved in the **ecumenical movement** of the whore of Babylon. The righteous people of God have absolutely nothing to do with the wickedness of the whore of Babylon.

Jesus-Christ is the only way to Heaven.

The seven heads of the beast

Revelation 17:9-10: "9 And here is the mind which hath wisdom. The **seven heads** are **seven mountains**, on which the woman sitteth. 10 And there are **seven kings**: **five** are **fallen**, and <u>one is</u>, and the <u>other is not yet come</u>; and when he cometh, he must continue **a short space**". (*See Rev 13:1-5*)

In order to identify those **7 kings** or **kingdoms** that are mentioned above, first of all, we will turn back to the prophecy of **Daniel 2:29**, and secondly, we will position ourselves in the time of the Apostle John. Let us not forget that this message was addressed primarily to *the 7 Churches of Asia*.

There are seven kings:

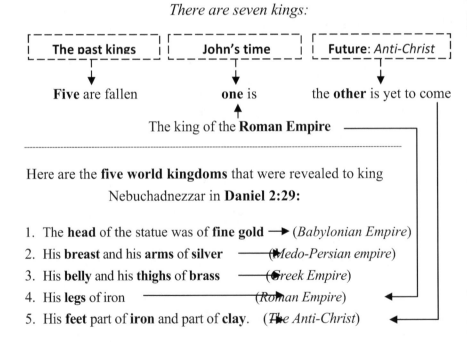

Here are the **five world kingdoms** that were revealed to king Nebuchadnezzar in **Daniel 2:29**:

1. The **head** of the statue was of **fine gold** ➝ (*Babylonian Empire*)
2. His **breast** and his **arms** of **silver** ——(*Medo-Persian empire*)
3. His **belly** and his **thighs** of **brass** ——(*Greek Empire*)
4. His **legs** of iron ——————(*Roman Empire*) ◄
5. His **feet** part of **iron** and part of **clay**. (*The Anti-Christ*) ◄

Let us not forget that the prophecy of *Daniel 2:29* was written before the prophecy of *Revelation 17:9-10*. The two kingdoms that are not mentioned on the list cannot be added neither *among* nor *after* **the five kingdoms** on the list, but they can only be added at the beginning. The only way we can truly identify the **two missing kingdoms** is by looking at the history of the nation of Israel in relation to each one of the **7 kingdoms** from Genesis to Revelation.

1. **Egypt** : 430 years of slavery followed by an annihilation attempt

2. **Assyria :** captivity of the northern kingdom of Israel (1 Chronicles 5:26)

3. **Babylonian Empire:** destruction of God's temple; 70 years of captivity

4. **Medo-Persian Empire:** rebuilding of the temple; Haman's slaughter attempt

5. **Greek Empire:** desecration of the temple of God; **Daniel 8:8-16**

6. **Roman Empire:** they crucified the Messiah; destroyed the temple in 70 **A.D.**

7. **The kingdom of the Anti-Christ:** It will persecute the children of Israel

Both the **Egyptian** and the **Assyrian** Empires were destroyed by the **Babylonian Empire** (*Jeremiah 28:14, 50:18, Ezekiel 29:17-20, 30:10, 30:24*-25). You can also read about the **Assyria Empire** in *Ezekiel 31*. Here is what happened to **Nebuchadnezzar's Army** before the world supremacy was transferred to his kingdom (**Jeremiah 37:5-7**):

"5 Then Pharaoh's army was come forth out of **Egypt**: and when the **Chaldeans** that **besieged Jerusalem** heard tidings of them, they **departed from Jerusalem**".

"6 Then came the word of the LORD unto the prophet Jeremiah, saying, 7 Thus saith the LORD, the God of Israel; Thus shall ye say to the king of Judah, that sent you unto me to enquire of me; Behold, **Pharaoh's army**, which is come forth to help you, shall return to Egypt into their own land. 8 And the **Chaldeans** shall come again, and fight against this city, and take it, and burn it with fire".

The **7th world kingdom** will have only **seven years** to repeat the abominable acts of its predecessors. The **dragon** with the **seven heads** will not change.

81

*The **first** and the **second** 3 1/2 years of the Anti-Christ*
(Revelation 17:8)

"**8** The beast that thou sawest **was, and is not,**

　| 　*Before the end of the **first** 3 ½ years, The Anti-Christ will receive a*
　|　*deadly wound. (Revelation 13)*
　↓

And shall ascend out of the bottomless pit,

　| 　*After his deadly wound is healed, the whole world will see him once*
　|　*again. (Rev 11:7, 13:1-5)*
　↓

And go into perdition:

　| 　*When he reappears on the world stage, he will be allowed to continue*
　|　*for another **42 months** or 3 ½ years (Rev 13:5).*
　|
　↓

"And they that dwell on the earth shall wonder, whose names were not written in the book of life from the foundation of the world, when they behold the **beast** that **was**, and **is not**, and **yet is**". (*Rev 13:3-4*)

Revelation 17:11

"11 And the **beast** that was, and **is not**, even he is the **eighth**, and is of the **seven**, and goeth into perdition".

The seven horns of the beast:

The **7ᵗʰ horn** of the beast represents the **Anti-Christ** (7ᵗʰ King)　　– – –↑

The **beast** that carries the **whore** also represents the **Anti-Christ** (*Rev 13:1-2*)

During the *first* 3 ½ *years*, the dragon will give his power to the Anti-Christ (the *7th king*), but when he reappears on the world stage at the beginning of the *second* 3 ½ *years*, he will be possessed by the dragon (*8th king*).

Revelation, chapter 18

The judgment of the whore of Babylon

When you are reading the details of this *eighteenth chapter*, please be reminded that all of those things were written in the context of the time of the Apostle John. This **satanic religious system** that has been established in the world since the time of the Roman Empire has greatly evolved over the years. The type of business activities that are described in the 18th chapter are no longer conducted in the same manner. The business activities of the whore of Babylon have now become more secretive.

Here is what the city of Babylon has become over the years:

Revelation 18: 1-2: "And after these things I saw another angel come down from heaven, having great power; and the earth was lightened with his glory. 2 And he cried mightily with a strong voice, saying, Babylon the great is fallen, is fallen, and **is become the habitation of devils,** and the **hold of every foul spirit**, and a cage of every **unclean and hateful bird**.

↑
Unclean spirits of the air

The only Holy man who is worthy to be acclaimed and worshipped by the creatures of God is the Lord Jesus. The only institution that is accredited by God to represent the Lord Jesus on the earth is the Church of Jesus-Christ. The harlot Church of Babylon has nothing to do with the Holy Church of God.

The whore of Babylon and all her accomplices will reap what they have been sowing on the earth over those past two thousand years. The Harlot Church of the queen of the second heaven will burn to ashes.

Revelation, chapter 19:

The bride of Christ and the glorious return of Jesus-Christ

The *Rapture of the Church* and the *glorious return* of the Lord Jesus have nothing secretive about them. The reason why the Church is not included in the events of the seven-year tribulation (*Revelation 6-16*), it's simply because she was not included in the **70 weeks of years** that were prophesied about the **children of Israel** and the **city of Jerusalem.** (*Daniel 9:24-27*)

"24 **Seventy weeks** are determined upon **thy people** and upon **thy holy city**, to *finish the transgression*, and to *make an end of sins*, and to *make reconciliation for iniquity*, and to *bring in everlasting righteousness*, and to *seal up the vision and prophecy*, and *to anoint the most Holy*".

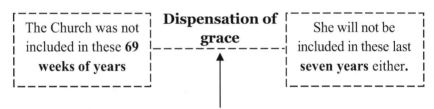

The Church was not included in these **69 weeks of years** — **Dispensation of grace** — She will not be included in these last **seven years** either.

The **Holy Spirit** and the **Church** will depart from the earth before the fulfillment of the *last seven years* of Daniel 9:27.

Revelation 22: 17: "And the **Spirit** and the **bride** say, <u>Come</u>. And let him that heareth say, <u>Come</u>. And let him that is athirst come. And whosoever will, let him take the water of life freely".

The **Rapture** of the **Church** will not be secret, but rather, it will be a **surprise** (*Matt 24:36*). The whole world will be aware of that event, but they will not understand it. Those who were against the Rapture will finally believe it.

The last three chapters that are not covered in this study do not really require any interpretation, because all of the events that will follow the judgment of the great tribulation are clearly revealed in the following order:

1. The return of the Lord Jesus, the battle of Armageddon, and the descent of the **Anti-Christ** and the **false prophet** into the lake of fire. (Rev 19)
2. The **chaining** and the **locking** of Satan in the bottomless pit (Rev 20: 1-3)
3. The physical resurrection of the great multitude that was slain on the earth (Revelation Rev 20: 4).
4. The Judgment of the nations (Matthew 25: 31-46, Revelation 20:4).
5. The **atonement** for the sins of the **remnant** of the children of Israel (Zechariah 3:9-10)
6. The building of the millennial temple (Ezekiel 40-48)
7. The enthronement of the King of glory in the city of Jerusalem

Psalms 24:7-10: "7 lift up your heads, O ye gates; and be ye lift up, ye everlasting doors; and the **King of glory** shall come in. 8 who *is* this King of glory? The LORD strong and mighty, the LORD mighty in battle. 9 Lift up your heads, O ye gates; even lift *them* up, ye everlasting doors; and the King of glory shall come in. 10 Who is this King of glory? The LORD of hosts, he *is* the King of glory".

At the end of the millennial reign of Christ (Revelation 20:7-14):

— Satan will be released provisionally for the fulfillment of his final act of wickedness before his final descent into the lake of fire.
— The judgment of the great white throne will take place
— Revelation 21: The Lord Jesus will establish a new creation

The book of Revelation is concluded with a warning from the Lord Jesus.

Conclusion

In such a time as this, it is absolutely paramount that we take some time apart to study the word of God for the benefit of our spiritual growth and for our doctrinal knowledge. The Revelation of the Lord Jesus was never given to the Church for the purpose of confusing or scaring God's people. If God didn't want to spare his Church from the Judgment of the great tribulation, he would not have revealed all of those things to his people in such a clear and detailed manner. The promise of the Rapture of the Church is a reality. The Church of Jesus-Christ will not fall under the judgment of God with the world. *If the whole world had accepted the Lord Jesus as their savior, we would not even hear about the coming of a great tribulation.*

The reason why God will judge the world, it is not because he takes pleasure in the suffering of his creatures, but it's simply because of their disobedience toward God. Even during the **first 3 $^{1/2}$ years** of the great tribulation, God will once again offer an opportunity to the world. He will send his angels to warn the world, yet they will still reject his forgiveness *(Rev 14:7-11)*.

Dear friend(s) in the Lord, the word of God is *clear*, it's *simple*, it is *self-sufficient*, and above all, it's *self-explanatory*. Keep reading it, keep trusting it, don't trust in your own wisdom, because the wisdom of God is better. May the Spirit of *truth* lead you in all the *truth* of God, and may the Lord strengthen your faith in his Son Jesus-Christ, our precious Lord.

Printed in the United States
By Bookmasters